I0221734

Christianity Is Better Than You Might Think

Christianity Is Better Than You Might Think

A Fellow Traveler's Guide to Reconsidering Faith

SO RI JUNG

WIPF & STOCK · Eugene, Oregon

CHRISTIANITY IS BETTER THAN YOU MIGHT THINK
A Fellow Traveler's Guide to Reconsidering Faith

Copyright © 2025 So Ri Jung. All rights reserved. Except for brief quotations in critical publications or reviews, no part of this book may be reproduced in any manner without prior written permission from the publisher. Write: Permissions, Wipf and Stock Publishers, 199 W. 8th Ave., Suite 3, Eugene, OR 97401.

Wipf & Stock
An Imprint of Wipf and Stock Publishers
199 W. 8th Ave., Suite 3
Eugene, OR 97401

www.wipfandstock.com

PAPERBACK ISBN: 979-8-3852-4788-2
HARDCOVER ISBN: 979-8-3852-4789-9
EBOOK ISBN: 979-8-3852-4790-5

VERSION NUMBER 041625

Scripture quotations are from the ESV® Bible (The Holy Bible, English Standard Version®), © 2001 by Crossway, a publishing ministry of Good News Publishers. Used by permission. All rights reserved.

For the seekers and skeptics, the firstborn and the prodigals
—may your journey lead you home

Contents

1

Reconsidering Christianity
At the Crossroads

It's dangerous to go alone! Take this.—Unnamed old man[1]

LET'S BE HONEST. YOU probably have an opinion about Christianity already. And if you're like many today, it's not a very flattering one. Perhaps you think of it as outdated, oppressive, or irrelevant—a relic of the past that no longer has a place in the modern world. Or perhaps you think it's a benign set of customs that can be a source of hope for individuals only when kept private. I'm writing in Australia, a Western country, in English, a Western language, in a Western culture that is increasingly post-Christian. Post-Christian, as in *after* Christianity.

Since the ascension of Christianity as the state-sponsored religion of the Roman Empire in the fourth century, it had been the default worldview—the lens through which one views the world—that governed the Western world. For nearly two thousand

---

1. Nintendo, "Legend of Zelda."

years, Christianity shaped art, education, politics, law, ethics, and culture.

But not anymore.

A few revolutions later—the Enlightenment, the Scientific Revolution, and now the Digital Revolution—we find ourselves here: a post-Christian world.

That is not to say we are *not* Christians. We are Christians still, but only *culturally*. One of the most famous atheists of our age, Prof. Richard Dawkins, recently sent shockwaves by saying that Britain is a culturally Christian country and that he calls himself a cultural Christian.[2] This is a culture that assumes a level of "Christianness" as a core value system—ideals like inclusiveness, mercy, and love—all the while conveniently removing the very foundation that supports these values. We live in a culture that wants to enjoy the fruits of Christianity while rejecting its roots.

It's also a culture that believes it knows everything there is to know about Christianity. After all, we've grown up surrounded by it—its symbols, traditions, and moral teachings. We think we've been there, done that, and are now able to make an informed decision to reject certain unsavory parts of it. But have we *really* understood Christianity? Or are we dismissing something we've only ever seen or heard second-hand?

As you engage with this resource, I invite you to keep an open mind. Imagine yourself walking down the path of life. You and I just happened to meet at life's crossroads. As a fellow traveler, I want to introduce to you the path I'm on. My goal is to help you see the path clearly, dispel the myths, address the objections, and uncover the heart of Christianity—its truth, goodness, and beauty.

Throughout the book, I will frequently use words like "maybe" or "perhaps." It's because important things need nuance, careful investigation, and a level of humility. I'm not *at* the destination calling you to come here but pointing *to* the destination so we can walk there together.

---

2. Leading Britain's Conversation, "Richard Dawkins: Cultural Christian," 0:26.

If you are a seeker, welcome! Thanks for picking up this book. Or, if you've left the church and deconstructed your faith but wish to reconsider Christianity, a very warm welcome to you, too! Or perhaps you are a Christian seeking inspiration on how to share the gospel with your friends. I'm glad you're here. Throughout the book, you'll see that I mentioned resources that have deeply influenced my thoughts. Feel free to explore them if you'd like to learn more. More importantly, I've quoted the Bible quite frequently. I encourage you to go to the source and see for yourself what the Bible says rather than just taking my word for it.

At the end of this short book, I hope you will see the beauty of Christianity that you had not appreciated before. Hopefully, you'll say, "Christianity is better than I had first thought."

2

Christianity Is More Reasonable Than You Might Think

But ultimately you have to deal, not with arguments, but with God himself.—William Lane Craig[1]

YOU MAY HAVE HEARD Christianity described as a "blind faith." It conjures an image of people covering their eyes, sheepishly following whoever's in front of them. To many, Christianity represents an outdated belief system that ignores modern, more rational, and scientific methodologies in search of truth.

This perception is widespread in our culture. Can you think of a time when, in movies, a Christian character was *not* portrayed as close-minded, unreasonable, or a bit dim-witted? Faith, we are told, is believing without evidence—or, worse, believing *despite* the evidence.

I know this perception exists because I feel it. I live through it. I have a PhD in biochemistry. I'm a Christian. When reading the last two sentences, you may have felt the urge to insert a "but" or

1. Craig, *Reasonable Faith*, 58.

4

a "yet" between them. That's how my scientist friends react when I tell them I am a Christian. Sadly, that's also how my Christian friends react when I tell them I trained to be a scientist. So, unfortunately, this perception exists on both sides.

But what if this picture of Christianity is wrong? What if the idea of "blind faith" is a caricature, one that doesn't accurately represent what Christianity has historically been or what it claims to be now? In this chapter, I want to suggest that the assumption that Christianity is unreasonable is, well, unreasonable.

Let's start with a bit of history.

Christianity and the Birth of Science

The claim that Christianity is hostile to science is one of the most persistent myths of today. The idea of scientific advances during the Enlightenment cutting through the religion-infested Dark Ages, stories about Galileo and the Inquisition, are frequently cited as evidence of this supposed tension. But there is another side to the story.

Far from being an obstacle to science, Christianity played a key role in its development. The scientific revolution—the birth of modern science—did not arise in a vacuum. It emerged in a cultural context essentially shaped by Christian theology, that is, the study of God. The Christian worldview provided the intellectual soil in which science could grow. Christopher Watkin says, "It was theological reasoning about the character of God that developed into scientific reasoning about the nature of the universe, and the wonder of modern science was born."[2]

Consider some foundational assumptions of science: the universe is orderly and governed by consistent laws that can be deciphered by rational minds. Pretty straightforward, right? Not quite. Many ancient cultures viewed the natural world as chaotic, unpredictable, or the result of impulsive actions by gods. Why is

---

2. Watkin, *Biblical Critical Theory*, 39.

there thunder and lightning? Zeus must be angry. Why is there a flood? Poseidon must be angry.

By contrast, Christian theology taught that the universe was created by a rational God who imbued it with order and purpose. As Isaac Newton, one of the most outstanding scientists in history, wrote: "This most beautiful system of the sun, planets, and comets, could only proceed from the counsel and dominion of an intelligent and powerful Being."[3]

I don't think it's an accident that many of the pioneers of modern science were Christians: Blaise Pascal, Gregor Mendel, and Francis Collins, to name a few. For them, studying the natural world was uncovering God's handiwork. It was an act of worship.

This is not to say that all scientists are Christians or that Christianity is the *only* worldview compatible with science. The polytheists in ancient Greece made great advancements in mathematics, and Islamic culture was the intellectual center of the world in the Middle Ages. The point I'm making is simply this: the idea that science and Christianity are fundamentally opposed is historically inaccurate. If anything, the birth of science owes much to the Christian conviction that the universe is orderly and worth investigating.

I should also mention that our current perception of Christianity against science, at least partially but quite significantly, owes to the rise of empiricism. Philosophers like David Hume (1711–1776) argued that only the type of knowledge derived from empirical tests—what we can test and verify with our senses—is truly valid. This shift toward empirical verification was highly influential not just in academia but also in public discourse.

But it's easy to see that we can't apply this framework universally because many aspects of human life—love, justice, beauty, and morality—can't be reduced to empirical tests.

For example, how do I know my wife loves me? Do I have the empirical methodology to determine it? Do I perform sentiment analysis on every conversation we have and determine with high

---

3. Newton, *Principia*, 619.

confidence that she is, in fact, still in love with me after five years of marriage?

How about the idea of fairness? We all want to be treated fairly, but what is the quantitative evidence that fairness is good? Should I send annual questionnaires to all people in a specific region to ask their opinions? What if fairness doesn't get the popular vote? Does it make moral values and duties subjective to the culture and community?

These are just a few examples, but you can easily find more. What values do you hold that are *purely* scientifically supported? I guarantee not many.

While empiricism has been a valuable tool, it cannot provide a comprehensive explanation of reality. Even the statement "all knowledge comes from empirical tests" cannot be empirically verified! That would require a database of *all* knowledge, valid empirical tests for each claim, and their results. That is absurd.

Also, while science excels at explaining the "how" of natural phenomena, it cannot address the "why." Why does the universe exist at all? Why do humans have a sense of moral duty? Why do we long for purpose and meaning in life? Strictly materialistic—the belief that everything is matter and there is no supernatural realm—frameworks often sidestep these questions, relegating them to the realm of subjective preference or dismissing them as unanswerable.

When reading science books or articles, see for yourself if the scientists are attempting to answer the "why" question. When they are, it's either a conveniently reworded "how" question, or they are not using science to answer the question.

Why do I love my wife? Depending on who you ask, scientists might respond, "because of high oxytocin levels" or "because love promotes bonding and cooperation, which ultimately leads to a higher chance of survival for your offspring who share your genetic materials." These are perfectly valid, scientific answers, but they do not answer the why but the how—the process by which the feeling of love is experienced and is beneficial. Science deals with *mechanism*, not *meaning*.

But the "why" questions are the ones that *truly* matter, aren't they? They are the ones we care about. We long for answers that aren't just intellectually satisfying but emotionally and spiritually fulfilling. Why is there something rather than nothing? Why am I here? It is not science but philosophy, religion, the arts, and literature that try to answer this question.

In this context, Christianity offers a thorough account of reality that integrates the everyday and the transcendent, the practical and the meaningful. It has done so for more than two thousand years.

Faith and Reason, Not Faith vs. Reason

So, where does this leave us? If Christianity fostered the growth of science, why is it often accused of being anti-reason? Part of the problem is a misunderstanding of what faith actually is in the Christian context.

The popular idea of faith as "belief without evidence" is not how the Bible defines it. In Christianity, faith is not a leap into the dark; it's a careful but confident step into the light.

The New Testament portrays faith as *trust based on evidence.* Consider the Gospels—the four biographies of Jesus by Matthew, Mark, Luke, and John—that record Jesus performing miracles, explaining how the Old Testament prophecies point to him, and inviting people to believe in him based on what they had seen and heard (see Matt 11:2–5 and Luke 24:25–27).

Interestingly, in the first chapter of the Gospel of John, Jesus is called the "Word" in English translations. In ancient Greek (the language it was originally written in), the word is *logos*, from which we derive the word "logic." Isn't it amazing that Jesus is called the "logic"?

Or think of Paul the apostle, who reasoned with Jews in synagogues, philosophers in Areopagus, and whoever passing by at marketplaces (see Acts 17:16–34), and apostle Peter, who said, "but in your hearts honor Christ the Lord as holy, always being prepared to make a defense to anyone who asks you for a reason for the hope that is in you; yet do it with gentleness and respect" (1 Pet 3:15).

See, faith is not opposed to reason but builds on it. It's the act of *trusting* in what you have good reason to believe is true. When you hear Christians say things like "I trust him even though I cannot fully understand," this is not an expression of blind faith. Instead, it's an expression of trust in Christ because he is reliable. When you know his existence, his goodness, and faithfulness, you trust him, even though you may not fully comprehend the *circumstances* that you are facing.

Please allow me to share a personal story. My wife, Eojin, and I were recently blessed with our little boy, Noah. But before this, we had a previous pregnancy that ended abruptly. Many people go through miscarriages, especially the early kind. I hear about one in five pregnancies end this way. Did I have this information? Yes. Did that give me any comfort? Not really.

Instead, it was our faith that God exists and that he is good that gave us the comfort and courage to start again. We don't know now and may never know why he allowed it to happen (Christians believe that everything happens under God's control). But we trust him. This is what we mean by "I trust him even though I don't fully understand."

Then how could I come to know God and his character to trust in him when everything else seems to have failed? What kind of evidence did I have? A full discussion would take an entire book (and then some), so let me very briefly touch on a few key pieces of evidence that I've found especially convincing for the existence of God. They are not proofs in the mathematical sense, but they are compelling *reasons* to believe that God exists; more and better reasons to believe than not to.

What I'm presenting here is but a taster, so if you want to learn more, I highly recommend William Lane Craig's *On Guard for Students: A Thinker's Guide to the Christian Faith.*

1. The Beginning of the Universe

Modern science tells us that the universe had a beginning. The Big Bang theory describes how the universe came into existence around 13.8 billion years ago. Everything that begins to exist has a cause. I came to exist. My cause is my parents. The universe began to exist. Therefore, the universe must have a cause. This simple yet effective argument was revitalized by a highly influential Christian philosopher, William Lane Craig, who terms it the *kalam* (referring to a school of medieval theology in Arabic) cosmological argument, acknowledging its historical roots in medieval Islamic thoughts.[4]

The argument doesn't just conclude that the universe has a cause. It also paints a picture of the cause that is remarkably similar to the theistic definition of God. As the cause of space and time, the cause itself must be beyond space and time. The cause must also possess great power, as it gave rise to all matter and energy. Lastly, the cause must be personal, as an impersonal cause must always coexist with the effect; that is, if impersonal, an eternal cause would have caused the universe for all eternity. We know that the universe is not eternal, so this implies that the cause consciously decided to create, therefore being personal.[5]

2. The Fine-Tuning of the Universe

When you look at the natural world, aren't you amazed? The trees, the wildlife, the mountains and rivers. And you wonder, "How is this possible?" The fine-tuning of the universe—the fact that the laws of physics are precisely calibrated to allow for life—is one of the most striking facts about the world. If the force of gravity were even slightly stronger or weaker, stars and planets could not form. If the cosmological constant were just a fraction different, the universe would have either collapsed in on itself or expanded

4. Craig, *Reasonable Faith*, 96.

5. Craig, *Reasonable Faith*, 152–53.

too quickly for galaxies to form. The odds of all these constants aligning by chance are astronomically low.[6]

How about in the fields of chemistry and biology? Origin-of-life researchers ambitiously claim that we can figure out how non-living matter can assemble itself into self-replicating, self-preserving life forms. But it turns out that even the simplest life forms are so complex, with hundreds of distinct proteins carrying out life-sustaining reactions, genetic materials that encode the said proteins, and the cellular capsule that protects them. It would take coincidences upon coincidences, miracles upon miracles, to even conceive of them all coming together at the same time by chance.[7] Even if it were possible, the building blocks and the physical laws that are required for such miracles would also need an explanation.

For many, the best explanation is that the universe was designed by an intelligent Creator.

3. Objective Morality

You would most likely agree with statements like: "Exploiting others for selfish gain is wrong," or "We ought to help others in need." We share many such moral values and duties, but where do they come from? If we are merely the product of blind evolutionary processes, why should we think that morality is real and not just an illusion created by our biology? If it's the result of random mutations and natural selection, why does it bind us? Or if it's just a social norm, and people should obey it, how come we celebrate the moral reformists who spoke out against the tyranny of their society?

Many find it more reasonable to conclude that our shared perception of objective morality points to a moral lawgiver. Just as human laws require authoritative lawmakers, moral laws require a transcendent source if they are to be objective. Christianity teaches that God is the source of all goodness, and our moral compass is

---

6. Craig, *Reasonable Faith*, 158–59.
7. See Rana and Ross, *Origins of Life*, 204–6.

a reflection of the Creator. Frederick Nietzsche describes the state we find ourselves in when we reject the objective lawgiver through one of his characters, the madman:

> We have killed him—you and I! We are all his murderers. But how did we do this? How were we able to drink up the sea? Who gave us the sponge to wipe away the entire horizon? What were we doing when we unchained this earth from its sun? Where is it moving to now? Where are we moving to? Away from all suns? Are we not continually falling? And backwards, sidewards, forwards, in all directions? Is there still an up and a down? Aren't we straying as though through an infinite nothing? Isn't empty space breathing at us? Hasn't it got colder? Isn't night and more night coming again and again? Don't lanterns have to be lit in the morning? Do we still hear nothing of the noise of the grave-diggers who are burying God? Do we still smell nothing of the divine decomposition?—Gods, too, decompose! God is dead! God remains dead! And we have killed him! How can we console ourselves, the murderers of all murderers![8]

We usually hear only the "God is dead" part of the quote from Nietzsche. But as the above, more contextualized excerpt indicates, he is describing the logical consequence of removing God from our discourse. When a tree is uprooted, how can we enjoy its fruits?

Of course, this is not the end for Nietzsche; in another work, he suggests that we can be lawgivers for ourselves, creating our very own moral values and duties. He says:

> Canst thou give unto thyself thy bad and thy good, and set up thy will as a law over thee? Canst thou be judge for thyself, and avenger of thy law?[9]

On the surface, this sounds uplifting and hopeful, but on a second glance, we realize this does not give us objective morality. It gives us a world each to their own.

8. Nietzsche, *Gay Science*, 119–20.
9. Nietzsche, *Thus Spake Zarathustra*, ch. 27.

This is exactly what happened in the garden of Eden, when the serpent said, "You will not surely die. For God knows that when you eat of it your eyes will be opened, and you will be like God, knowing good and evil" (Gen 3:4–5). You may know the rest of the story: Adam and Eve fell into the temptation and ate from the forbidden tree, deciding for themselves what was right or wrong, not accepting the only rightful lawgiver, God.

By the way, why do you think Nietzsche used a *madman* to say these words? Maybe, and I'm being speculative here, he remembered this Bible verse:

> The fool says in his heart, "There is no God." They are corrupt, they do abominable deeds; there is none who does good. (Ps 14:1)

4. The Bible

The Bible often gets brushed aside as just an ancient book full of myths and outdated ideas. But despite what some people may think, it's one of the most influential books in history. Its unique nature, historical reliability, and the way it changes lives make it a key reason why Christianity is more reasonable than one might assume.

The Bible isn't just one book—it's a compilation of sixty-six books written over thousands of years by various authors from all sorts of backgrounds: kings, scholars, prophets, fishermen, and shepherds. Despite this diversity, it tells one unified story about God and humanity. This kind of consistency is pretty extraordinary.

It also explains so much about what we observe in life—about meaning, purpose, morality, and what comes next. Some of these questions include:

1. Why does the universe exist? The Bible says it is not an accident but a purposeful creation by a loving God (Gen 1:1).

2. Why do we matter? The Bible says that we're made in God's image, which gives us intrinsic value (Gen 1:27).

3. Why is there so much pain and suffering in this world? The Bible points to humanity's free rebellion against God as their cause (Rom 5:12–14 and Rom 8:18–23).

4. What's our ultimate purpose? According to the Bible, our purpose is to know, love, and glorify God (1 Cor 10:31 and Rom 11:36).

The Bible provides a comprehensive framework that helps us make sense of the world and our place in it. C. S. Lewis famously said, "I believe in Christianity as I believe that the Sun has risen, not only because I see it, but because by it I see everything else."[10]

In a sense, this is quite *scientific*. Just like a scientific model, the Bible provides a model through which we can provide explanations, make predictions, and subsequently evaluate them in light of our observations.

For example, I can make a prediction that some nations will start yet another war in the not-so-distant future. Why? The interpretative model from the Bible tells me that everyone is a sinner, and a fundamentally *human* endeavor to enlighten or enhance society doesn't work. That's why Jesus had to come. That's why he has to come again. This prediction has proven itself time and time again.

I can also predict that despite the pain and suffering, despite all the reasons to be pessimistic, we will find hope and compassion. There will be a flood of non-government organizations trying to help those in conflict zones despite the imminent dangers. Why? The interpretative model from the Bible shows that everyone bears an image of God. Even though the image is shattered, there are pieces of the image that shine through the darkness. Self-sacrifice, love, compassion, and mercy are core values for all of us. This prediction has also been shown true time and time again.

The historicity of the Scriptures (another word for the Bible) and the fulfilled prophecies are also worth our attention. The Old Testament has tons of predictions about a coming Messiah (also called Christ, which means the anointed one or the chosen one),

10. Lewis, "Is Theology Poetry?," 15.

many of which line up perfectly with the life of Jesus. For instance, Isaiah wrote about a suffering servant who'd bear the sins of many (Isa 53)—and he did this seven hundred years before Jesus was born.

When speaking about the historicity of the Scriptures, I can't fail to mention Jesus's resurrection. His resurrection powerfully confirms his identity as the Son of God and is, therefore, an essential foundation of our faith. Paul said, "And if Christ has not been raised, your faith is futile, and you are still in your sins" (1 Cor 15:17).

The New Testament texts were written during the lifetimes of those who saw the events firsthand, giving us accounts that can be tested under historical examination. The resurrection story is also consistent across the four Gospels, with the authors' unique takes, which adds to its credibility.

We also notice how the apostles changed completely after the resurrection. They went from being terrified and in hiding (see John 20:19) to boldly sharing their faith despite persecution (see Acts 4:1–21). Put yourself in their shoes for a moment. Their leader had been executed by capital punishment. If they had fabricated the story of the resurrection, why would they risk their lives proclaiming it?

I've heard people argue against this point, saying that religious zealots die for *the cause* all the time. But the important difference here is that if the disciples had faked the resurrection, they would have *known* it was a farce; the modern-day religious zealots don't! This drastic change tells us that something amazing must have happened.

There is a lot more to say about the reasonableness of believing in Jesus's resurrection, but I'll keep it short and recommend a book for further investigation. Lee Strobel's *Case for Christ: A Journalist's Personal Investigation of the Evidence for Jesus* is a great introduction to this fascinating topic.

But the proof is in the pudding, right? One of the most convincing things about the Bible is how it changes people. Countless people over thousands of years have shared how the Bible changed their lives. It freed people from addictions, inspired them to fight for justice against all odds, and brought hope in the darkest situations. Slave traders became abolitionists, and violent gang members became pastors. If you have a Christian friend, ask them: How has the Bible changed their lives? Chances are, they will give you an answer in a heartbeat.

Of course, more can be said about the relevance and impact of biblical teachings in our lives, so we will take a closer look at this topic in the next chapter.

Conclusion

Imagine yourself as a juror in a court. The trial is about to begin, and the judge tells the jury, "No matter what the prosecution tells you, you can *never* conclude that the victim was murdered." Now, that would be highly inappropriate, right? You would instead be asked to follow the evidence wherever it may lead you.

This brings us back to the idea of faith.

In Christianity, faith is not believing *despite* the evidence but trusting *in light of it*. It's the reasonable response to what we know about the world and about God. Christianity may believe in the supernatural, but it is not anti-natural. Childers and Barnett put it this way (emphasis original):

> So are faith and reason in conflict? It depends entirely on how one defines faith. Faith as active trust based on evidence is certainly not at odds with reason. Reason *assesses* whether or not a belief is true and then faith trusts in *that belief* in light of those reasons.[11]

Jesus, the *logos*, does not demand a blind faith. He gave us plenty of reasons to believe and place our trust in him. Faith in Jesus is not an anxious leap into the dark but a confident, *reasonable* step into the light.

This, of course, doesn't mean that faith eliminates the need for doubt or struggle. Just as our trust in a scientific fact (e.g., the

---

11. Childers and Barnett, *Deconstruction of Christianity*, 175–76.

beginning of the universe) is enhanced as it withstands the test of time and counterarguments, our confidence in Christ is enhanced *through* doubts and struggles. Not only in the academic sense but also in the inevitable struggles in life—losses, pains, and unrealized dreams—Christians discover that Jesus is faithful, and our faith in him is warranted.

3

Christianity Is More Relevant Than You Might Think

So what?—Christopher Watkin[1]

IF YOU SEE A high school student doing their mathematics homework, I can guarantee you would hear them complain: "What's the point? When am I ever going to use this in real life?"

We often hear the same for Christianity.

Maybe, at this point, Christianity makes sense to you. You may not fully agree with its internal logic, but you at least see where we are coming from. Or maybe you are convinced by the evidence I presented in the previous chapter and think that there might be some truth to Christianity. But so what? How is this relevant in your life?

Christopher Watkin puts it this way (emphasis original):

> Let's take one example. We are taught what the final judgment is. We may well be taught how to explain it to others with some rather quaint analogies and illustrations, and

1. Watkin, *Biblical Critical Theory*, 2.

perhaps we are taught how to defend and justify it. But we are less frequently—at least in my experience—taught what difference it makes to politics, to the sciences, to the arts, or to the possibility of knowledge about anything at all. We are taught the "what?" and the "why?" but not so much the "so what?" The same goes for the "so what?" of sin, judgment, promise, covenant, law, prophecy, exile, incarnation, the cross, resurrection, ascension, the last days, and the final things. *So what* for human beings? *So what* for society, for our hopes, fears, and deepest values? *So what* for art, for justice, for history, for the environment? These biblical truths, and many more besides, have far-reaching consequences in all these areas. And what is more, these consequences often bring a fresh and constructive perspective to bear on the abiding social and cultural questions of our day.[2]

Many today are asking this question: *So what?* Let's talk about it.

Christianity and the Big Questions

Why are we here? Where are we going? From the beginning, we have asked these questions through philosophy, religion, the arts, and literature. How can I say "from the beginning" when our written records don't extend that far? Well, because we have discovered burial sites that date back as early as eighty thousand years ago.[3]

Fast-forward to today. Despite the numerous attempts by New Atheism and Scientism (the belief that science is the only way to know the truth), we are still asking these questions. Stoicism is enjoying its newfound revival in the popular space; self-help books with elements of spirituality are always at the top of the sales chart in bookshops. While the Western world is celebrating its "graduation from religions," almost 90 percent of the world's population is projected to be religious by 2050.[4]

2. Watkin, *Biblical Critical Theory*, 2.
3. Martinón-Torres et al., "Earliest Known Human Burial," 95–100.
4. Pew Research Center, "Global Religious Futures Project."

But what if we had the answers all along? What if Christianity provides a comprehensive account of reality, in a relevant, meaningful way?

1. We Are Made

The Bible begins with the words "In the beginning, God created the heavens and the earth" (Gen 1:1). Maybe you've heard this too many times to appreciate it, but this was a big bang (figuratively, but also maybe literally!) that changed everything.

The contemporary cosmogonic (study of the origin of the universe) model to the book of Genesis was the ancient Babylonian creation myth, *Enuma Elish*, and this gives us a unique insight into what people at the time believed. It describes that the universe came about as an afterthought following a bloody conflict between the gods.[5] In stark contrast, Genesis presents the creation event as a planned, ordered, deliberate act of God.

A parallel can be drawn in response to the much more modern materialistic views on the creation of the universe. Naturalists may not like this conclusion, but their worldview has the same implication as *Enuma Elish*: that we are *an accident*.

Among Christians, there is a diversity of thoughts on *how* God created. Did he use evolution as a natural mechanism to create diverse life? If so, did he also use natural mechanisms to assemble chemicals into life? These are good questions with deep philosophical implications, but what all Christians agree on is this—*that* God created.

And if we are created, then we have a purpose. I write this book with a purpose. The computer that I'm typing from was made with a purpose. Whenever something is made, it has a purpose, a reason it was created for. By contrast, if we were an accident, we don't. There is no direction in which we are going.

Remember Nietzsche's story I shared earlier? Existentialist philosophers like him accept the implication of non-design, that

5. Dickson, "Purpose of Genesis 1."

life is ultimately meaningless and directionless. In this view, the big questions we asked earlier, "Why are we here?" and "Where are we going?" are absurd.

Instead, they would say things like, "How beautiful is it that we can *create* meaning for ourselves?" and "How noble!" But is it truly beautiful and noble? Who decides what is beautiful and noble? Is it not the individual with no objective ground to stand on? What if what I find beautiful and noble differs from what someone else thinks?

No wonder Nietzsche was opposed to the idea of equality.[6] You don't have to trust me or the expert I just referenced unquestioningly, however. Just listen to what Nietzsche himself says:

> For thus speaketh justice UNTO ME: "Men are not equal." And neither shall they become so! What would be my love to the Superman, if I spake otherwise?[7]

And how could we be equal if we were just accidents? There will be people who rise above the challenge of the absurd and make and enforce rules for themselves (Nietzsche calls such a person Übermensch, which is translated to Superman in the quote above). And there will be those who thoughtlessly follow those currently in power. How could we rate them equally on Nietzsche's "nobility scale"? See, the consequence of believing we are just accidents isn't just *personal*. It has a broad *societal* impact.

By contrast, Christians believe that we are created. So what? To be created means to be bound. Bound by the creator's design. If I make a shoe, I create it with a purpose and with a design. The shoe cannot one day think being a shoe is beneath them (pun intended) and decide that it would rather be a hat and have all the spotlight. That would make a great Pixar movie, but you get the point. A shoe is to be used as a shoe. It does not belong on top of someone's head.

Is that limiting? Not at all! To tell a boy that he cannot be anything he wants when he grows up is helping him understand

---

6. Wilson, "Nietzsche and Equality," 212.

7. Nietzsche, *Thus Spake Zarathustra*, ch. 29.

reality. We know the boy cannot be a dinosaur, no matter how bad he wants it.

When we say God created us, we acknowledge the unique right of the creator. He sets the rules. He sets the design.

And what was the design he had for us? The Bible says, "So God created man in his own image, in the image of God he created him; male and female he created them" (Gen 1:27).

There have been historical debates about what this image of God (*imago Dei* in Latin) is, but it's now broadly accepted that it's not just an attribute or a quality of a human being, like intelligence. If it were, then we would have yet again a worldview that discriminates based on the degree to which someone has an image of God. For example, if someone has an IQ of 120, he is more God-like than someone with an IQ of 100. That is absurd.

Instead, we now understand the image of God in man as this: a *representative*.

Have you ever been to a temple? A temple typically has a statue of a god—an idol. Adherents of such religions bow before the idol because it represents their deity. In the same way, the declaration that we are made in the image of God means that we were created to represent him in this world.[8]

That is our identity infused to us by the Creator. That is the unique value that all humans have, by virtue of being human. All our other identities, like ethnicity, gender, and culture, are secondary. Genesis doesn't say that in the beginning, God created Africans and Caucasians. It says that God created *man*—humanity.

Biblical scholar David J. A. Clines says (emphasis original):

> That is to say, man is defined according to the divine summons of Genesis 1:26 which is constitutive for man's being, as "the image of God," a term which denies any fundamental quality to the phenomenal difference between man and man. Man everywhere is *essentially* the same. Every distinction between man and man is

---

8. Peterson, "Image as Identity," 69.

secondary to the fundamental standing of every man as the image of God.[9]

The idea we are made in the image of God gives us the toolkit to treat everyone *equally* despite how broken the image is.

2. We Are Broken

What do I mean by broken? I will detail the idea of sin and its relevance in the next chapter, so I'll be brief here. We were created as the image of God, his representatives. But we felt that was beneath us. Why reflect someone else's light when you yourself can radiate?

This is at the heart of the temptation, "For God knows that when you eat of it your eyes will be opened, and *you will be like God*, knowing good and evil" (Gen 3:5; emphasis added). You may say, "Oh, but that's Adam and Eve; I wouldn't have fallen into that temptation," but we do—*every day*.

We want to be the center of the universe. We defend our selfishness and pride disguised as personal autonomy and freedom. We cry, "It's not fair!" when it's inconvenient for us, and look the other way when there are actual instances of injustice. We are champions of inclusion and tolerance as a society but cannot tolerate anyone who disagrees with us personally.

The problem is that we are not created that way.

Just as any created object can break when it's not used according to its intended purpose and design (imagine how much you need to cut open a shoe to wear it on your head), when we deviate from our design, we break.

Picture a mirror. When a mirror breaks and shards are scattered, we no longer see things clearly. It loses its function. But sometimes, some pieces are bigger than others, and you see a glimpse. This is how it's with the image of God in us. Despite the brokenness, shards of his image reflect his glory. We see beauty in creation and hope in humanity not because it's perfect but because it was created "good" despite the corrupting effects of sin.

9. Clines, "Image of God in Man," 94.

Sin isn't an arbitrary concept that makes people feel morally inadequate. Instead, it accurately describes the existential shame and guilt we all face every day.

No amount of money, power, or status in the world can make you immune to this charge. It doesn't matter if you are a politician, billionaire, or celebrity; we all say, "I'm not good enough." Here lies the relevance; it's a great *equalizer*. It provides a toolkit for us to truly be inclusive. We are all in this together, so let's be nice to each another.

3. We Have Been Saved

Church father (early Christian theologian whose writings shaped Christian doctrine and practice) Athanasius says:

> What then was God to do? Or what should be done, except to renew again the "in the image" so that through it human beings would be able once again to know him? But how could this have occurred except by the coming of the very image of God, our Savior Jesus Christ? For neither by human beings was it possible, since they were created "in the image"; but neither by angels, for they were not even images. So the Word of God came himself, in order that he being the image of the Father (cf. Col L.15), the human being "in the image" might be recreated.[10]

Athanasius goes on to make this analogy: If a portrait is destroyed, how can we restore it without the original figure it was based on?[11]

Jesus is the very image of God. He said, "Whoever has seen me has seen the Father" (John 14:9). He is the image of God that truly fulfilled its functions. He was sinless, obedient, and authoritative, reflecting God's glory here on earth. But having an example to follow is not enough—our hearts are corrupt. It's not just that

10. Athanasius, *On the Incarnation*, 63.
11. Athanasius, *On the Incarnation*, 63.

we don't *know how*; it's that we *don't want to*. We must be made anew. We need a fresh start.

But there is a problem. Our rebellion against God requires punishment. He cannot just forgive without justice being fulfilled because if he did, he wouldn't be a just God. At the same time, the punishment should be proportionate to the crime. If I steal a loaf of bread, I should be punished. If I assault a person, I should be punished to a greater degree because the value of the loaf of bread and that of a human being is incomparably different.

Now, the nature of our sin is rebellion against God. God created the universe—we are in his world. We wanted to be gods in his place. What is the value of his name and authority that we defiled? If we were to be proportionally punished, how could a mere mortal bear the punishment so severe? What is the punishment deserving of us who tried to overthrow the king?

Apostle Paul says, "The wages of sin is death" (Rom 6:23). Not just a physical death, but an eternal, spiritual death, away from God's presence and his goodness.

Here lies the problem. For God to fulfill his justice, we should be punished. But we are weak and cannot bear the punishment proportionate to our crime. What was God to do?

This is why the cross stands at the very heart of our faith. It's the symbol of Christianity! Just think about how strange that is for a moment. The cross was an execution method, the most brutal kind. Most religions wouldn't use the way its founder has died as the religious symbol, right? But we do in Christianity because it marks the moment when Jesus bore the penalty for our sins. As God, Jesus had the divine strength to carry the weight of the punishment deserving of our sins, and in his humanity, he represented us. On that cross, God's perfect justice and his boundless love came together.

The resurrection that followed proved Jesus's divine nature and innocence. Now, whoever trusts him enjoys the benefit of this sacrificial death and the hope of resurrection one day.

But what does that mean for us today? In other words, *so what*?

When I was nine years old, my cousins and I were playing at a public swimming pool, and despite not being a great swimmer, I decided to go to the deep end. If you've ever struggled in deep water, you know the panic. Time passes by slowly; seconds feel like an eternity. Then, out of nowhere, someone reached in and pulled me out into safety. I couldn't rescue myself; I clung to the one who saved me.

That's what happened when Jesus pulled us out. He pulled us out when we had no way of saving ourselves.

And once you've been saved, you don't just go back to drowning. In my story, I didn't just say thank you to the lifeguard and dive back into the water the next minute. You live *differently* because you've experienced rescue. You try to avoid sin not to *earn* salvation but because his grace has already saved you.

We are saved from sin; we are saved from *ourselves*. We are freed from the constant temptation of ego, the evolutionary urge of self-preservation, and the never-ending search for self-fulfillment.

The idea that God would forgive us of our sins, not because of our own doing but because of his own mercy, puts us back in our place. We are *totally* dependent. We are *completely* reliant. We cannot stand on our own. All we can say is "Thank you."

So, what is there to compare ourselves with how other people are doing? What use is there in being anxious about being good enough? Paul says, "For by grace you have been saved through faith. And this is not your own doing; it is the gift of God, not a result of works, so that no one may boast" (Eph 2:8–9).

4. We Are Being Saved

But salvation isn't a one-time event—it's an ongoing process. Paul says, "For the word of the cross is folly to those who are perishing, but to us who are *being saved* it is the power of God" (1 Cor 1:18; emphasis added). God continually works in us, shaping us to become more like Jesus.

Salvation isn't about getting a pass to heaven. It's not ticking a box. It's about *real* transformation in the *here and now*. It changes how we think, how we treat others, and how we live our daily lives.

And let's be honest—it's not always easy. It would be naive to view the human condition, especially the Christian one, to say that the job's finished. Even pastors give into sexual temptations and have excessive and luxurious lifestyles, flying the world in private jets. Pastors are easy targets, but looking more broadly, how many self-identifying Christians have you seen that do not hold up the values and duties that Jesus commanded, like love your God and love your neighbor (Mark 12:30–31)? Those who *use* Christ's name for their own political and business gain rather than to be *used by* him.

The gravitational pull of the self is strong. Very strong. And when I give examples of others' behaviors, I'm not counting myself out. How many times have I lied to my bosses for their approval, telling myself that it's not a big deal? How many times have I given in to temptations even after becoming a Christian, despite having the necessary toolkit to overcome them?

Change takes time. We still mess up. It's like an old habit—a force of inertia that's hard to stop in its tracks instantly. But the good news? We're not left on our own. Jesus said, "But the Helper, the Holy Spirit, whom the Father will send in my name, he will teach you all things and bring to your remembrance all that I have said to you" (John 14:26). The Holy Spirit actively works in us, helping us fight sin, grow in love, and live purposefully.

5. We Will Be Saved

While being saved, we await our salvation with hope and anticipation. The promise of Jesus's return signifies the fulfillment of God's plan for humanity. When Jesus returns, he will restore the world to the way God planned it to be—with God's presence and ruling being felt and experienced (see Rom 8:18–25 and Rev 21:1–8).

So, Christians can remain hopeful even when everything seems to be going wrong. There are geopolitical tensions and environmental issues, and neighbors turn on each other based on race and ethnicity. The hope of Jesus's return gives us the toolkit to see beyond this mess and look forward.

That doesn't mean we *don't* act here and now. With God's help, we do what we can to prepare the way for the Lord. After outlining how we will be glorified and made anew in the end, Paul says:

> *Therefore*, my beloved brothers, be steadfast, immovable, always abounding in the work of the Lord, knowing that in the Lord *your labor is not in vain.* (1 Cor 15:58; emphasis added)

The logical implication of Jesus's return is not *inaction* but *action.*

Christians don't say, "Jesus will come and make everything better, so we just have to sit back and wait." We say, "Jesus will come and make everything better, so my work here now has meaning and purpose. It won't be in vain."

Applying the Principles

There is much more to say, but hopefully, this gave you a taste of how the Christian worldview provides an invaluable framework for making sense of it all. Christian living is, then, essentially learning and practicing to *apply* it in every corner of our lives. From the way we treat each other, care for the environment, process our own emotions and desires, and, yes, even the way we vote and participate in public discourse. Believing in Christianity isn't signing up for an insurance policy so that you can get to heaven when you die. Instead, it radically transforms the way you view life here and now.

Here is a story about how this happened to me.

I was born in a Christian family; my dad is a pastor. My dad wasn't one of those megachurch pastors you would see on TV or YouTube, but it came with his occupation that his family was also on the pedestal. I had to attend every church service and event. If you know Koreans or are one, you know how intense we get.

Back in my day (I'm not that old; it's the change that happens so quickly), even more so. There were early morning prayers every day, Wednesday night services, Friday night prayers, and Sunday schools.

Looking back, it's not that big of a deal, but to me, then, it was a huge deal. I had to be there and be seen. I wanted, no, *needed* that recognition, that praise. This naturally translated to how I approached schoolwork and, of course, also how I thought about God. I needed his recognition; I needed his praise. But there was a problem. Nothing that I could do would be enough. He watches our hearts with fiery eyes, right? He sees me when I'm alone, right?

That bugged me. That annoyed me. In all honesty, that *scared* me. I didn't want to disappoint God, but it felt like nothing I did would be enough. But how could I hide from him? Should I just hope he doesn't exist like my friends were telling me?

Then, one day, I discovered the good news: "but God shows his love for us in that while we were still sinners, Christ died for us" (Rom 5:8).

And this truth set me free.

That was the end of my search for recognition and acceptance. If God accepted me for who I am—when I was still a sinner—and if God demonstrated that love on the cross, what more can I do to *earn* his favor?

This principle still guides me today. When I'm tempted to embellish my accomplishments, I think about the cross. When I'm tempted to work too hard to be "that guy," I remember the cross. When I'm tempted to boast about the stuff I own, I remember the cross.

If I have already been accepted, not because of what I've done, but because of God's love for the undeserved (this is the technical definition of the word "grace"), then I no longer have to search for anyone else's acceptance. If I were friends with Tim Cook, I wouldn't be too concerned about whether the staff at the Genius Bar liked me or not. Likewise, when I have received God's acceptance, why thirst and long for anyone else's?

My story isn't as supernatural or awe-inducing as others. I have heard many amazing stories about how people become Christians. However, I share my story nonetheless for one purpose alone: to show that my belief in Christianity has a *real impact* on the way I live. It's not "I believe in Jesus, so when I die, I'll go to heaven." That's the irrelevant Christianity that many have rejected.

Jesus said, "The kingdom of God is in the midst of you" (Luke 17:21). When someone walks with Jesus, we enjoy the benefit of heaven here on earth. Yes, we long for the kingdom of God to come in its fullness, but we are enjoying the foretaste here. Right now.

Another story, this time not mine. A few years ago, I found myself in Cambodia on a missions trip. There, I met this young man, our translator. This is his story.

If you know something about Cambodia's history, you know it's dark. Very dark. Khmer Rouge (1975–1979), a communist regime led by Pol Pot, utterly ransacked the nation, responsible for the genocide of three million people.[12] Pol Pot, under the influence of socialist ideals, wanted to make the country an agricultural society, so the primary targets were anyone with an education. In this process, they employed child soldiers.

My new friend's father was one of the child soldiers. Of course, he was just following orders, but once the regime failed, his photo was posted publicly, along with all his fellow soldiers.

Then, there was a revenge attack on his house, and his mother was killed. His father remarried, and his stepmother didn't treat him well, so he left and lived alone. Now, with the help of a missionary, he found God, and he is at peace.

There are more stories like this everywhere in the world. Christianity has helped mourning parents overcome the death of their children and convicts repent of their ways and become missionaries in foreign lands. It has also helped people beat addictions and anger issues. Christianity *works*.

---

12. Editors of Encyclopaedia Britannica, "Khmer Rouge."

Conclusion

Of course, the fact that it works doesn't necessarily make it true. It could be a placebo effect where you believe in the effect of a drug so much that it works, even if it were a sugar pill. Or you might think Christianity is a fictional reality or an imagined order, as sociologists would call it. In that view, Christianity works because people hold onto the belief and operate on that basis, enhancing cooperation and keeping order. That doesn't make it *true*.

However, there are many reasons to believe Christianity is true, such as the beginning of the universe, the fine-tuning of the universe to support life, objective morality, and the reliability of the Scriptures, a topic I explored in the previous chapter.

What's important is taking all the evidence together. When you do, you'll find that Christianity is the *truth* that *works*. It's the *truth* that is *relevant*.

By this point, you already know that I'm a new dad. As an inexperienced dad, there are times when I don't quite get what Noah needs. One day, I tried to feed him with a bottle, and he refused. If you have a child (or more) of your own, you also know that this isn't a polite refusal. He cried, he pushed the bottle away, he was waving his arms and legs, literally kicking and screaming. It turns out he wasn't hungry; his nap was overdue. As soon as I gave up on the feeding and put him on my shoulder, he fell asleep.

Sometimes, Christianity feels like this. You have your immediate needs, but Christianity seems far off. You hear all the religious jargon like being born again, salvation, and redemption, but you don't see how that would make a difference in *your* life.

What I'm suggesting is this: Christianity is not an abstract concept that has no bearing on your life. Christianity flips a switch in a dark room and helps us make sense of it *all*—why we feel so ashamed, why everything seems to be falling apart, and why we can still find hope despite all the reasons to be pessimistic.

I hope you discover the relevance of Christianity, as many have done for thousands of years. Christianity is *true* and is *relevant*.

4

Christianity Is More Inclusive Than You Might Think

We can't do this alone. We are very much dependent on others. We therefore also have a moral obligation to help each other in the search for truth.—Elmer John Theissen[1]

CHRISTIANITY AND INCLUSIVITY; MAYBE these two words don't go well together in your vocabulary. In recent years, Christianity has been framed as an exclusive, bigoted, intolerant belief system. Much of it is owing to what Christians have done (and I'm sorry if you've been at the receiving end of this), but others are due to certain fundamental misunderstandings about what Christianity is about. There are quite a few things to get through, and I want to start with what it means when Christians say we have the truth.

---

1. Thiessen, *Ethics of Evangelism*, 148.

Truth, not Preference

I love mint chocolate flavored ice cream. I'm told that some people simply cannot stand it, saying it tastes like toothpaste. And I'm shocked. I cannot let this hatred go unchecked, as mint chocolate is the best ice cream flavor. I tell all my friends we cannot be friends anymore if they disagree. I surround myself with only those who believe in the same "truth" as I do. I declare that all the unbelievers will be judged accordingly.

This, unfortunately, seems to be the way people think Christians act. Indeed, there are so many worldviews and religions out there. Why act as if Christianity is the only truth? Even if you *prefer* Christianity over everything else, why force that *preference* on others? This would be a fair criticism if Christianity claimed only to be a preference. But let's see if that is the case.

Imagine a sinking ship like the *Titanic*. Debris from the ship—pieces of wood, doors, and inflatable life jackets—is floating around. People hold on for their dear lives. The night is deep, and everyone is getting cold.

Suddenly, you see a light. It's a big lifeboat. Someone from the boat throws you a rope, and you let go of whatever you are holding onto and grab onto the rope instead. You get on board, change into dry clothes, and are welcomed by the captain and the crew. You know you're safe and sound, but then you realize your friends are still floating in the ocean. You say, "What are you doing? Grab onto the rope!" And their response, "I'm comfortable here. Let me hold onto this piece of wood and swim back to shore. I *prefer* it here."

If you are a loving friend, you would tell your friends that that wouldn't be a good idea. You don't know where you are; it's dark out there, and hypothermia is a serious business. Wouldn't you say, "Please come to your senses! You can trust the captain, the boat, and the rope. And you certainly can trust me. There are no other options; just grab onto this rope and be saved!" Would anyone criticize you for being too exclusive and intolerant? Forcing your preference on others?

In the same way, all the Christian beliefs I shared in the previous chapters are truths, not mere preferences. Our belief that God created the universe is not a preference, nor is the belief that God is the objective lawgiver. Likewise, the belief in the historicity of Jesus's resurrection is also not a preference. If these beliefs were preferences, we wouldn't require evidence and reasons to examine them. Instead, we believe these statements to be true.

Not *true* in the sense of "Speak *your* truth" or "What's true for *you* may not be true for *me*." I mean truth, in the *objective* sense—existing independently of personal preferences or cultural contexts. The gospel claims the truth about God, our awful state, and salvation. If these claims are objectively true, Christians have the moral obligation to share this truth for the benefit of others. Philosopher Elmer John Theissen says:

> We can't do this alone. We are very much dependent on others. We therefore also have a moral obligation to help each other in the search for truth. If therefore I believe something to be true, then I have a moral obligation to try to persuade those around me to accept my position. Interestingly, in bio-medical ethics it is generally conceded that a physician has a moral obligation to try and persuade a patient to adopt a solution to his or her medical problem that the physician believes to be the best for the patient. A politician has a moral obligation to propose and persuade voters to adopt policies that he or she believes will contribute to the common good. Of course, another politician of different political persuasion might disagree and try to persuade voters of the opposite. And may the best argument win! Both politicians, if they are genuinely caring people, will (and should) try to persuade voters of their position.[2]

But you might think that's a bit arrogant to say *you* have the truth! Theissen says, "We have here also an explanation as to why the charge of arrogance is made against proselytizing. Proselytizers

2. Thiessen, *Ethics of Evangelism*, 148.

assume that they have the truth. They further proclaim their truth as something that everyone should believe.[3]

Maybe you've heard of the story of six men with visual impairment figuring out what an elephant looks like. Each man touches a part of the elephant and claims to know the truth about the animal, when in reality, each is only experiencing a small part of the whole truth. The moral of the story is that no one can claim to know *the truth*.

But do you know who knows the truth in the story? The storyteller! To claim that *no one* has the objective truth requires *some* knowledge of the truth. The person looking at the six men *saw* the elephant in its entirety. That's how he knew they didn't have the full picture.

So, it's not the Christian who is arrogant in claiming he has the truth—the charge should be made against the critic. If you want to say there is no truth, you have to provide evidence for that, but in order to do that, you have to claim to know the truth. It goes in circles, never resolved. This is a self-refuting argument with a hint of pride.

One more thing.

Christians believe in objective truth, but not just *any* objective truth. It's the objective truth *that matters*. We discussed this in more detail in the previous chapter, so here, I want to simply say this. Sure, bananas are berries, but strawberries aren't. This is a fact, an objective truth. Objective truth in the sense that it's factually correct whether I like it or not (it's very confusing to call strawberries berries if they are, in fact, not berries!). But I don't go out of my way to pour my heart out to a stranger to convince them to believe it. Instead, I might occasionally use it at parties if I want to head home early.

Christians share our beliefs in the objective truths that *matter*—that have life-defining, life-changing, and life-saving implications.

We believe that we are created by a benevolent, powerful God and that we are broken because of our failure to follow the created

3. Thiessen, *Ethics of Evangelism*, 59.

design and purpose. We believe that Jesus is the only way to re-store the way things ought to be. And because we believe that these statements are objectively true, we have the moral responsibility to tell others about them because of their implications. People's lives depend on it.

By way of an example, if I see a woman with visual impair-ment walking into oncoming traffic and I don't warn her, won't I be morally responsible? This obligation is articulated in the Bible: "If I say to the wicked, 'You shall surely die,' and you give him no warning, nor speak to warn the wicked from his wicked way, in order to save his life, that wicked person shall die for his iniquity, but his blood I will require at your hand" (Ezek 3:18). But I don't have to quote the Bible to convince you—you would agree that it would be right to warn her.

And precisely because it's morally right, the idea that one possesses an objective truth related to survival can sometimes lead to forceful techniques. In the above example of a visually impaired woman walking into oncoming traffic, no one would expect me to take my time to carefully persuade her in hopes she would *choose* to stop in her tracks. Instead, I would be expected to use *some* force to stop her immediately, grabbing her arms, for example. In-deed, who could blame a paramedic for breaking a few rib bones while performing CPR to save a person?

No doubt this was the reasoning used by Christians and other religious proponents as they adopted coercive conversion tactics throughout history, such as Charlemagne's baptism by the sword.[4] These days, coercion takes more psychological forms. After a se-ries of interviews with forty-two American millennials who left the Christian faith in their adult life, Taylor noted:

> The vast majority of my interviewees were not able to exude agency over their socialization into this highly controlled ideology. However, when the individuals I in-terviewed moved away from their family of origin home environments, they were able to enact small amounts of agency, and it was at that time they realized they could

4. Thiessen, *Ethics of Evangelism*, 79.

question the prescriptions that had been forced upon them.[5]

These exemplify the disastrous attempts of *very* misguided Christians to bring others to the truth. I can say they are misguided because, unlike the examples above of helping a visually impaired person or performing CPR, Christians are told that *we* are not the saviors; *Jesus* is.

I loved talking to people in my twenties (I still do!) and did a lot of street evangelism. I went up to people who were hanging out in public squares, asking if they had the time to talk about faith. If and only if they said yes, we talked. I didn't force my belief on them; I didn't force them to come to church with me. We just talked because belief cannot be forced.

Christians are called to lovingly share the good news of Jesus and trust the Holy Spirit to touch your hearts, mend the wounds, and awaken your souls. We are *not* called to do a power play (political or otherwise) and force others to believe our way or else. Paul says:

> And the Lord's servant must not be quarrelsome but kind to everyone, able to teach, patiently enduring evil, correcting his opponents with gentleness. God may perhaps grant them repentance leading to a knowledge of the truth, and they may come to their senses and escape from the snare of the devil, after being captured by him to do his will. (2 Tim 2:24–26)

Labeling coercion as unethical *is* legitimate, and Christians should *absolutely* reject such methods. If you have been at the receiving end of such coercive evangelism techniques, I'm very sorry. That's not what we were meant to do.

What About Other Religions?

I live in Australia, a very multicultural nation. I have neighbors who are Muslims, and I have colleagues who are Hindus. Some of

5. Taylor, "Deconstruction and Disidentification," 66.

my friends are atheists, and others are "spiritual." In this melting pot of cultures, can Christians claim that Christianity is superior to other worldviews?

Some of this has been covered in the chapter "Christianity Is More Reasonable Than You Might Think," but a few more things can be said here.

First, there is a reasoning process called "inference to the best explanation," where you conclude that a particular hypothesis is most likely true because it provides the best explanation for a set of observations or evidence compared to other possible explanations.

Using this principle, we can evaluate the different worldviews. The intricate design of the universe, the co-existence of so much good and evil in people, the seemingly endless conflicts and the failure of so-called solutions, and the feelings you get when you go out in nature: awestruck and amazed. There are acceptable, competing models to explain all these observations. Our task, then, is to assess which is the best and, therefore, most likely to be the truth—you might have already guessed what my conclusion is.

Second, we have to reframe our thinking when Christians say, "We have the truth." Oftentimes, I hear people talk about many different ways of getting to the top of a mountain. Yes, if you're hiking through a tiny hill in your backyard, sure, there might be infinite routes. But you can imagine that the higher and the more dangerous the mountain is, the fewer options we'll have.

Now, which mountain are we talking about when we consider religious choices? We are talking about the *mountain of God*. The Greeks called it the Olympus, and the Chinese called it the Kunlun. How can we, mere mortals, reach the peak of the divine? Haven't we failed repeatedly after thousands of years of searching and trying?

Christianity isn't saying there is only one path to the top of the mountain of God, and that happens to be our religion—an arbitrary rule set from a position of power. Instead, we are saying there is *no* way. We are all in this together. We are all corrupt, and none of us know the way. The mountain is so high and so dangerous that no one can reach the peak. The Bible says, "for all have sinned and fall short of the glory of God" (Rom 3:23). Because of this situation we find ourselves in, there is no other choice but to rely on the one who is *indigenous* to the mountain. The Son of God, Jesus Christ.

He is the one who felt pity for us and came down from the mountain. He is the one who met us where we were, on the outskirts of the mountain, given up and defeated. He is the gate, he is the way, he is the path. Our duty now is to trust him, hold onto his hands, and follow his footsteps. That's what we mean by Jesus is the only way.

Even among the so-called Christians, there are those who relish the political and cultural power that Christianity enjoys, not really following his path. Jesus says, "Not everyone who says to me, 'Lord, Lord,' will enter the kingdom of heaven, but the one who does the will of my Father who is in heaven" (Matt 7:21).

You're Calling Me a Sinner!

This brings us to the thorny subject of sin. At the center of apparent or actual Christian exclusivity today lies the topic of sin. So, what is sin?

1. Sin as a Breakage of Shalom

Philosopher Cornelius Plantinga Jr. describes sin as "culpable shalom-breaking."[6] According to his view, *shalom*, or peace, is "the way things ought to be."[7] Sin breaks the way it's supposed to be and, therefore, results in negative consequences that the Creator has not intended for his creatures.

Maybe an analogy will help.

Let's say you buy a microwave oven, and it comes with a safety manual from the manufacturer. The manual says, "Do not place a metal object in the microwave when operating." You do not

---

6. Plantinga, *Not the Way*, 14.

7. Plantinga, *Not the Way*, 10.

take this warning seriously and put your metal spoon in the oven along with your plate of food. What happens when you turn on the microwave? Imagine this: Your phone suddenly rings. It's the CEO of the manufacturing company. He says, "I have given you an explicit warning, but you did not listen. I have no choice but to destroy your machine in five . . . four . . . three . . ." Now, this would be ridiculous. The microwave will malfunction because it was not used as it was supposed to.

God is often portrayed as a dictator who wields arbitrary rules against his very own creation. However, in this view, sin and the resultant punishment are consistent with the view of a Creator who created an ordered world with consistent application of natural laws.

This is the context in which Christians view certain lifestyles as sinful. As an example, we believe that sex outside of marriage, i.e., the holy union between a man and a woman, is a sinful act because it's not the way it's supposed to be and because breakage of this design principle leads to consequences that are contrary to the fulfillment of our purpose. In this context, calling something sinful is *recognizing* that brokenness.

Yes, some Christians have applied this principle in a holier-than-thou attitude, drawing the line between "us" and "them," the "saints" and "sinners." Their favorite Bible verse is, "Or do you not know that the unrighteous will not inherit the kingdom of God? Do not be deceived: neither the sexually immoral, nor idolaters, nor adulterers, nor men who practice homosexuality, nor thieves, nor the greedy, nor drunkards, nor revilers, nor swindlers will inherit the kingdom of God" (1 Cor 6:9–10). They say to themselves, "Phew, thank God I'm not one of them."

But Jesus says, "Whoever says, 'You fool!' will be liable to the hell of fire" (Matt 5:22), and "everyone who looks at a woman with lustful intent has already committed adultery with her in his heart" (Matt 5:28). With this high bar, who could be free from guilt and shame?

Christianity recognizes that we are *all* broken and in need of a Savior. There is no "us" and "them," no "saints" and "sinners." We are *all* sinners.

Think about what this idea does. It levels the playing field. It's the great equalizer. Do you have sex outside of marriage? Yes, you're a sinner. Do you run a profiteering business? Sinner. Do you gossip about your coworkers? Sinner. Do you "follow your heart" at the expense of those around you? Sinner. There are many, *many* more ways this common condition is expressed. No one is exempt.

A common cold virus can infect two different people and result in two different sets of symptoms. One might have dry coughs, while the other gets a fever and runny nose. Christian exclusivity is like the "dry coughs" patients shunning the "fever and runny nose" patients. We all have the same virus.

Christianity is more inclusive than you might think. And not *despite* the idea of sin but precisely *because* of it. Christians don't *tolerate* sinners; we *identify* with them. We *are* them.

2. Free Will and Sin

You might agree with what I said so far but still have an issue with the definition of sin as *culpable* shalom-breaking. If we are born this way, how can we be responsible? Didn't God make us this way?

Let's explore this with an analogy. Imagine you're born into a family burdened by debt. You didn't create the debt, but it affects you. You grow up under its weight, and your opportunities are shaped by it. The Bible teaches that humanity's "debt" is a result of sin—not just individual symptoms but a deep, spiritual condition we're all born into. This idea is often called "original sin," which is recognizing a brokenness that permeates everything—a brokenness we inherit, like debt.

So, do we just blame our ancestors? Put yourself in the shoes of Adam and Eve for a second. When presented with the opportunity to "be like God" (Gen 3:5), would you have done otherwise? Can you say with confidence that you wouldn't have fallen into that temptation? This is precisely what we do every day—wanting to make and play by our own rules. We want to be the master of our destiny; no matter what others say, we want to *follow our hearts*. Isn't that exactly what Adam and Eve did? Can we blame them?

We can discuss all day and night concepts like libertarian versus compatibilist freedom of the will (a very important topic that needs serious attention), but the bottom line is this: we are free agents. We perceive ourselves and act accordingly. We have no one else to blame.

3. God's Wrath and Hell

Now, we come to the topic of God's wrath. In the analogy of the microwave I shared earlier, the manufacturer is not *angry* at the purchaser for not following the safety manual. In real life, they wouldn't even know.

By contrast, in the Bible, especially in the Old Testament, its authors regularly depict God as angry. For example, when a man named Zimri usurped the throne of Israel and destroyed the whole family of Baasha, the then-incumbent dynasty, we read:

> Thus Zimri destroyed all the house of Baasha, according to the word of the LORD, which he spoke against Baasha by Jehu the prophet, for all the sins of Baasha and the sins of Elah his son, which they sinned and which they made Israel to sin, provoking the LORD God of Israel *to anger* with their idols. (1 Kgs 16:12–13; emphasis added)

Yes, we face the natural consequences of the breakage of sha-lom—the way it's supposed to be. That's true, but it's also true that rather than being a God of deism who created the universe and left it to its natural course, Christians believe in a *personal* God.

But God's wrath often makes people uncomfortable because it feels incompatible with the idea of a loving God. Isn't God supposed to be merciful?

Here, it's important to understand that God's wrath is not a volatile, emotional outburst but a righteous response to sin and injustice. Think of it this way: If you deeply love someone, you are bound to feel anger when someone harms them or if they harm themselves or others around them. God's anger arises *because* he loves us and hates the ways sin destroys his creation.

The manufacturer of the microwave doesn't feel anger because they have nothing to do with you. By contrast, fathers care deeply about their children and their well-being. Imagine if a child deliberately ignored safety instructions and suffered harm as a result. Any loving parent would feel a combination of grief, frustration, and even righteous anger—not because they hate their child, but because they long for their child's good.

Similarly, God's wrath is tied to his justice. Justice is an essential part of love. We live in a world where people often cry out for justice when wrongs are committed. Think about the most gruesome crimes and deliberate acts of injustice—don't we want those who commit such acts to be held accountable? Doesn't it give us comfort to believe that those criminals who got away from human laws will never get away from God's? Don't we say things like "He'll get what he deserves" to console victims of crime? What do we mean by that if we don't believe in the concept of divine judgment? God's justice *ensures* that evil does not go unchecked. His anger against sin reflects his commitment to *set things right*.

This brings us to the uncomfortable topic of hell. Many people imagine hell as a fiery torture chamber, an imagery that Christians use to scare kids into behaving. Hell is an unjust, unfair, and imbalanced punishment for minor crimes, they say.

At its core, hell is the ultimate separation from God. The Bible says, "They will suffer the punishment of eternal destruction, *away from the presence of the Lord* and from the glory of his might" (2 Thess 1:9; emphasis added).

If that is the case, isn't that precisely what we have been longing for? To wash away our guilt and shame, to remove the concept of sin, haven't we dreamed of a world where God, the objective lawmaker, does not exist? Doesn't our popular culture portray hell as a fun place with no rules and no boundaries? If that is the case, how is it unfair that we are getting what we have been asking for?

Pastor Timothy Keller describes hell as:

God actively giving us up to what we have freely chosen—to go our own way, be our own "the master of our
fate, the captain of our soul," to get away from him and
his control. It is God banishing us to regions we have
desperately tried to get into all our lives.[8]

God does not force anyone into a relationship with him. Hell
is the tragic result of choosing to reject God and his ways entirely.

Hell is but a natural extension of life's trajectory. We are already living the effects of hell, aren't we? The seas are warming,
nations are waging wars, and neighbors are turning against each
other. Imagine this life being extended for eternity, as you've
longed for, minus God, whom you took for granted. There will be
no objective values and duties, no end to your spiritual longing,
and no sense of beauty and awe. That's a horrible state to be in.

So, it's timely to note that the Bible *consistently* portrays God
as reluctant to execute judgment. God declares, "I have no pleasure
in the death of the wicked, but that the wicked turn from his way
and live; turn back, turn back from your evil ways, for why will you
die, O house of Israel?" (Ezek 33:11). And God "desires all people
to be saved and to come to the knowledge of the truth" (1 Tim 2:4).

And God would be a just God even if he left us in our path,
saying, "You asked for it!" But no, God did something about it. He
decided to send his only Son, Jesus Christ. He bore our debt when
he was cursed on that cross in our stead. And his resurrection was
proof that he is indeed the God he said he was.

Paul says, "But God shows his love for us in that while we
were still sinners, Christ died for us" (Rom 5:8). While we were
still unlovable, he loved us. While we were still cheerfully running toward hell, he loved us. While we rejected him and rebelled
against our Creator, he loved us. While we were still his enemies,
he loved us. Loved us to the point of Jesus dying for our sins.

---

8. Keller, "Importance of Hell," para. 13.

Conclusion

Christians are more inclusive than you might think because we understand the objective truth about our shared human condition.

Lusting after others online, numbing ourselves with endless scrolling, envying a friend's promotion or a stranger's "perfect" life on social media, harboring resentment toward those who have wronged us, cutting corners in business to maximize profits, lashing out in anger at strangers on the road—these are but a few of the countless outward expressions of our shared underlying problem: sin.

We live in a broken world, far from the way things ought to be. And no one stands above the other. The fact that sin is expressed differently gives no one the grounds to exclude or reject. We are all in this together.

Just as the bad news is for everyone, the good news is for everyone. Jesus invites *all* who labor and are heavy laden to come to him (Matt 11:28). All are welcome. Come to him as you are, and you'll discover God has already started the work of restoring *shalom*—the way you are supposed to be. The way God has meant you to be.

5

Christianity Is More Diverse Than You Might Think

After this I looked, and behold, a great multitude that no one could number, from every nation, from all tribes and peoples and languages, standing before the throne and before the Lamb, clothed in white robes, with palm branches in their hands, and crying out with a loud voice, "Salvation belongs to our God who sits on the throne, and to the Lamb!"—Rev 7:9–10

WE HAVE AN INTERESTING situation. On the one hand, Christianity is getting a bad reputation for being too uniform. White nationalism, imperialism, and colonialism are some of the bad "-ism" words often ascribed to Christianity in this context. It's the "white" religion, some say.

On the other hand, however, Christianity is often criticized for being too diverse. Some say there are now more than forty-five thousand denominations of Christianity.[1] "If Christianity is the truth, why are there so many disagreements?" people ask.

1. Johnson, "Christianity Is Fragmented," para. 1.

So, which is it? Is Christianity too uniform or too diverse?

Keen readers would have noticed that my previous characterization of the charge of uniformity relates to a lack of *cultural* diversity, whereas the charge of diversity pertains to a lack of *doctrinal* unity. These are the two primary areas we will discuss in this chapter, but first, it's important to outline the Christian foundation that underlies this discussion.

Christian Answer for Unity and Diversity

Unity and diversity aren't mutually exclusive in Christianity; in fact, they're inseparable. Even if you're not (yet) a Christian, you would have heard the famous saying "God is love." This appears in a letter sent from John, Jesus's disciple. In its context, this is what he said:

> Beloved, let us love one another, for love is from God, and whoever loves has been born of God and knows God. Anyone who does not love does not know God, because God is love. In this the love of God was made manifest among us, that God sent his only Son into the world, so that we might live through him. In this is love, not that we have loved God but that he loved us and sent his Son to be the propitiation for our sins. Beloved, if God so loved us, we also ought to love one another. No one has ever seen God; if we love one another, God abides in us and his love is perfected in us. (1 John 4:7–12)

The logic is beautifully simple. Christians are to love one another because God is love, and love is from God. Anyone who knows God cannot *not* love others.

So, if love is such a big deal for God, it makes you wonder: Who was God loving before he made us? Did God only *start* loving once we showed up? That makes it sound like God *needed us* to *gain* something that he was missing, like God wasn't *God* before the creation. A god that depends on its creation—that doesn't sound like, well, *God*, does it?

Christians believe that even before we came into the picture, there was already perfect love between the Father, the Son, and the Holy Spirit—the Trinity. They are one God but three distinct persons, which can be a bit mind-boggling, I know. But I'm not going to bother with analogies to make it make sense because there is truly nothing like this in the universe. Using analogies like the solid, liquid, and gaseous states of water or three leaves of clovers have problems, and it confuses more than it clarifies.

The important takeaway is that God was complete before anything else was created. God was loving before us, merciful before us, and God was *God* before us.

The idea of the Trinity is the very foundation for the Christian understanding of unity and diversity. We believe in one God, who is many, ultimate unity in essence but diverse. We believe that this same God invites us to share in this beautiful harmony of unity in diversity.

Wilkin and English say:

> At the heart of the Christian life is a communing fellowship with each person of the Trinity. The fellowship enjoyed between the three Persons for all eternity invites you to partake in its riches.[2]

The idea of unity and diversity is ingrained in the core of Christianity. The world's diversity isn't an accident; it reflects who God is.

Christianity: The Religion of Diversity

I'll be honest. When I first heard the narrative that Christianity is a "white" religion, it surprised me. I was also surprised to hear white nationalists hijacking the Christian message to further their agenda. Yes, there is a rich history of Christianity in Europe and North America that cannot be downplayed, but the narrative that Christianity is "white" needs to be challenged, not because it's inconvenient, but because it's simply untrue.

2. Wilkin and English, *You Are a Theologian*, 45.

To understand the true nature of Christianity, we must start at the beginning. And it doesn't begin in North America or Europe; it begins in the Middle East.

Jesus was born as a Jew in Judea under Roman occupation. As someone with Korean heritage, this resonates with me quite deeply. Even though I haven't experienced it firsthand, history has taught us about the horrors of the Japanese annexation of Korea. Koreans were treated as second-class citizens or worse. Of course, it's not possible to draw too much from this comparison, but the point I want to make is this: Jesus was far removed from privilege.

He was born into an oppressed people group, the Jews, living under Roman rule. Unlike Roman citizens who had birthrights and protections, Jesus—like many in his time—had none of that. That's why, when he was falsely accused, tortured, and sentenced to death by the worst execution method ever invented, he was not given a fair trial.

But Jesus didn't come to lead the Jews out of the Roman rule, to overturn the social order, to the disappointment of many. John the Baptist sent his disciples from prison to ask, "Are you the one who is to come, or shall we look for another?" (Matt 11:3). Now we can only imagine the frustration and doubts that would have plagued John when he was sitting in prison. He had preached that the Messiah (the chosen one) was coming soon to judge, so people should get ready. Now, Jesus was here, but he wasn't gathering armies or making political gestures.

Instead of overturning the social order, Jesus came to tear it all down. Apostle Paul puts it this way: "For he himself is our peace, who has made us both one and has broken down in his flesh the dividing wall of hostility" (Eph 2:14). The gospel isn't about elevating one ethnicity or one nation over the others—it's about breaking down the divisions.

I should also note that while understanding Jesus's background helps us appreciate the cultural context, it wasn't the core part of who he was. We don't praise and worship Jesus *because* he was oppressed and marginalized. We don't praise and worship Jesus *because* he wasn't white. We praise him because he is the Son of

God, our King who saved us from tyranny, regardless of his earthly ethnicity and social status.

In the same way, when we place our trust in Jesus, our focus and our priority in our identity change. Paul says, "So you are no longer a slave, but a son, and if a son, then an heir through God" (Gal 4:7).

Jesus is the Son of God. When we trust in him, we are united with him (see 2 Cor 5:17, Rom 8:9–11). And in him, we are adopted into the family (Rom 8:15). That's what makes Christianity so powerful—our identity is now primarily that of God's children. My identity as his son comes before my ethnicity, nationality, gender identity, or anything else.

I should also mention that when Paul talks about us being "sons," he isn't ruling out women. He preached the gospel to women and men alike and ministered with female colleagues. On the contrary, when he uses the gendered language here, he is being radically inclusive. Timothy Keller puts it this way:

> Many take offense at using the masculine word "sons" to refer to all Christians, male and female. Some would prefer to translate verse 26: "You are all children of God" (as the NIV 2011 does). But if we are too quick to correct the biblical language, we miss the revolutionary (and radically egalitarian) nature of what Paul is saying. In most ancient cultures, daughters could not inherit property. Therefore, "son" meant "legal heir," which was a status forbidden to women. But the gospel tells us we are all sons of God in Christ. We are all heirs. Similarly, the Bible describes all Christians together, including men, as the "bride of Christ" (Revelation 21:2). God is even-handed in his gender-specific metaphors. Men are part of His Son's bride; and women are His sons, His heirs. If we don't let Paul call Christian women "sons of God," we miss how radical and wonderful a claim this is.[3]

No doubt, the egalitarian nature of the gospel contributed to the explosive expansion of Christianity. It didn't matter if you were an Ethiopian eunuch (Acts 8:26–40), a Roman centurion

3. Keller, *Galatians for You*, 90.

(Acts 10:1–48), a businesswoman (Acts 16:14–15), a slave girl (Acts 16:16–18), a philosopher (Acts 17:18–34), or a king (Acts 26:1–32); the good news was shared.

Now, the rest is history. Christianity flourished in various regions, including Nubia, Ethiopia, and Egypt in Africa, where it deeply influenced local cultures.[4] By the seventh century, it even spread to the Tang Dynasty in China.[5]

What contributed to the spread of Christianity is its adaptation to different cultures while remaining faithful to its core message. For example, while Western art often depicts Jesus as a bearded European figure (maybe this is what you're used to seeing in popular media), in Ethiopia, he is portrayed with African features. In China, early Christian writings used familiar local concepts to explain biblical teachings.

As another specific example of this adaptation, Jesus often uses bread as a metaphor (see John 6:35). When the Bible was translated into Korean, the translators chose to adapt rather than introduce a foreign food that locals were unfamiliar with. The Western staple was transformed into an indigenous food, *tteok*, rice cake, all the while preserving the core message.[6]

Of course, we cannot deny that Christianity is intricately tied to European history, including the period of imperialism, but it's overly simplistic to label it a "white religion." If anything, wouldn't this demonstrate the accuser's Eurocentric bias?

Consider also the trend in Christianity today: The number of Christians in Asia, Africa, and South America has exceeded that in North America and Europe.[7] The center of Christianity has shifted to the Global South. Countries like China, Nepal, and Cambodia are seeing rapid growth in the number of believers despite government restrictions and persecution. South Korea, once a missions field, has become one of the world's largest senders of missionaries.

4. Africa Study Bible, "History."

5. Morris, "Rereading the Evidence," 253–54.

6. Kim, *Translations in Korea*, 40–42.

7. Zurlo et al., "World Christianity and Religions," 78.

This global nature of Christianity is a testament to its unity. Though Christians worship in different languages and cultural expressions, they share the same gospel, the same Christ, and the same hope. Christianity is not confined to any one nation or tradition—it's a faith that welcomes people from every background, inviting them into the family of God.

Christianity: The Religion of Unity

When I first came to Australia, I remember having a nice little chat with an elderly gentleman who was then my neighbor. I don't know how we got on this topic, but we were discussing my faith as a Christian. Then he asked me, "Oh, are you an Anglican?" At that point, I had never even heard that term before (the Anglican church wasn't very big in Korea). I simply replied, "No, I'm a Christian!"

One of the most common criticisms of Christianity is that it's fragmented. With so many denominations—Baptist, Pentecostal, Methodist, Presbyterian, and many more—some people assume that Christianity is divided beyond repair. It wouldn't be a stretch to suggest that this criticism has contributed to the significant decline of mainline denominations and the reciprocal growth of nondenominational churches (churches that are not affiliated with any specific denomination) and churchgoers in the United States.[8]

But this assumption misses something crucial: Christianity is far more united than it might seem. In fact, the diversity of denominations doesn't weaken Christianity; it strengthens it.

To understand why Christianity remains a religion of unity despite its many denominations, we must recognize the difference between core and secondary beliefs. Core beliefs are the essentials—the key truths that truly define what Christianity is all about. Remove those, and Christianity becomes, well, not Christian.

By contrast, secondary beliefs are important, but they don't determine the essence of the church. Now, I'm *far* from the ultimate

---

8. Cachiaras, "Movement Away."

authority on deciding which belief falls into which category. As a Protestant, I reject such human authority! Certainly, there will be disagreements and debates, but that's part of the diversity, isn't it?

C. S. Lewis writes:

> I hope no reader will suppose that "mere" Christianity is here put forward as an alternative to the creeds of the existing communions—as if a man could adopt it in preference to Congregationalism or Greek Orthodoxy or anything else. It is more like a hall out of which doors open into several rooms. If I can bring anyone into that hall I shall have done what I attempted. But it is in the rooms, not in the hall, that there are fires and chairs and meals. The hall is a place to wait in, a place from which to try the various doors, not a place to live in. For that purpose the worst of the rooms (whichever that may be) is, I think, preferable.[9]

What are these core beliefs that would get you to the "hall," as Lewis puts it? I can name a few: the authority of Scriptures, the creation out of nothing by the Triune God, the full deity and humanity of Jesus and his saving works on the cross and his resurrection, our salvation through faith in him alone, the continuing works of the Holy Spirit in us, the importance of the church, and the second coming of Jesus.

On the one hand, these core beliefs unite Christians from all denominations. Whether one is Presbyterian, Baptist, or Pentecostal, these foundational truths remain unchanged. They make us Christians.

On the other hand, secondary beliefs differ between denominations and churches. These include the way we perform baptism, church governance, our understanding of free will, worship styles, and many others.

These differences are significant. There is a reason I'm not a Pentecostal but a Presbyterian! But these differences do not make me reject my Baptist and Anglican brothers and sisters in Christ. They do not change a Christian's core identity. Instead, they show

---

9. Lewis, *Mere Christianity*, xv.

that Christianity allows room for discussion, growth, and adaptation across cultures and historical contexts.

Christianity is not a one-size-fits-all religion. It has thrived across different continents, languages, and cultures, adapting to new environments while staying rooted in the gospel.

Denominations exist because Christians are diverse. People worship in different ways, emphasize different aspects of theology, and organize their churches differently. But at the end of the day, these differences do not change the gospel itself.

Yes, when secondary beliefs are elevated or core beliefs compromised, we face issues—real division. I'm not denying that such things occur; they certainly do, and rightfully so! For example, the sixteenth-century Reformation was a time for real division when the practices of the Roman Catholic Church at the time did not align with Christianity's core beliefs. Even today, we have faithful colleagues writing and speaking against organizations that, in the guise of Christianity, advance self-serving causes.

The point I'm making here is that what makes Christianity unique is that it does not demand *uniformity* to maintain *unity*. Christianity makes room for different expressions of faith while keeping the main thing—Jesus.

This very idea is also evident in how the individual books of the Bible relate to one another, especially the four biographies of Jesus—Matthew, Mark, Luke, and John. They were written by different people with specific audiences in mind. There are details that differ among the books, and these differences *enhance* their reliability rather than diminish it. If they were identical, the uniformity would suggest that they are not independent accounts but merely copies of one another. Instead, the differences in secondary details, but their unity on the main events, lend more validity to these books as historically accurate accounts.

Unity is not about agreeing on everything—being *uniform*. It's about *being one* in Christ. And that is precisely what has happened throughout church history. Despite differences in tradition, practice, and culture, Christians worldwide are still proclaiming the same gospel, worshiping the same Savior, and sharing the same hope. Paul explains this point beautifully in this analogy:

> For just as the body is one and has many members, and all the members of the body, though many, are one body, so it is with Christ. For in one Spirit we were all baptized into one body—Jews or Greeks, slaves or free—and all were made to drink of one Spirit. For the body does not consist of one member but of many. If the foot should say, "Because I am not a hand, I do not belong to the body," that would not make it any less a part of the body. And if the ear should say, "Because I am not an eye, I do not belong to the body," that would not make it any less a part of the body. If the whole body were an eye, where would be the sense of hearing? If the whole body were an ear, where would be the sense of smell? But as it is, God arranged the members in the body, each one of them, as he chose. If all were a single member, where would the body be? As it is, there are many parts, yet one body. (1 Cor 12:12–20)

The uniqueness and the distinctiveness of each part of the body *enhance* the unity of the whole. Enforcing uniformity for its own sake is not only counterintuitive but also detrimental. Voth and Muller say:

> Christianity is a global family. There are believers on every continent, and, if we truly believe that we are one part of many in the body of Christ, we need each other. We can't look at another location or culture and say, "I don't need you." The Bible is God's revealed truth to the world, and we gain new perspectives when we look at Scripture through the eyes of others.[10]

When Christians embrace diversity, we do not just embrace a culture or a people group; we embrace and celebrate the richness of God's truth that he has revealed to us.

---

10. Voth and Muller, *Living in the Text*, 25.

Conclusion

One of the places I've loved visiting as a street evangelist is Auburn in Western Sydney. My fond memory of the place is not just about the fruitful conversations and amazing food but also the friendship I enjoyed with the local church there, whose congregants were mainly Christian refugees from conflict zones. They were from the Middle East, from Africa, and from all over the world. They maintained their cultural distinctiveness and worshiped the same God in unquestionable unity. This multicultural worship is something that reminds me of a particular passage in the Bible:

> After this I looked, and behold, a great multitude that no one could number, from every nation, from all tribes and peoples and languages, standing before the throne and before the Lamb, clothed in white robes, with palm branches in their hands, and crying out with a loud voice, "Salvation belongs to our God who sits on the throne, and to the Lamb!" (Rev 7:9–10)

The book of Revelation details a series of visions that John saw about the end times. There is a lot of intriguing symbolism and mysteries in the book, but this is by far my favorite scene. People "from every nation, from all tribes and peoples and languages" worshiping together is what we are looking forward to as Christians.

Christianity is diverse but united. We are diverse in areas that we should be, like language, culture, nationalities, and ethnicities, and united in areas that we cannot compromise: our core beliefs about who God is, who we are, and our salvation in Jesus alone.

Diversity and unity do not contradict each other in Christianity. We believe God is both one and many. And we believe we are called to be a unique part of the body of Christ, embracing and celebrating diversity, which *enhances*, not undermines, our unity.

In Christianity, diversity is not a checkbox to tick—it's who we are.

6

Christianity Is More Awesome Than You Might Think

So go ahead and stare dumbstruck for a while at the magnificent otherness of God on display in his world and his word. Don't worry about how small it makes you feel. Embrace it. For small is what you are.—Adam Ramsey[1]

CHRISTIANITY IS AWESOME. YES, in the sense of being admirable and nice, just like when you win in a video game. But more than that, in the original sense of the word, it's *awe-inspiring*.

What is awe? The *Merriam-Webster* dictionary defines it as "an emotion variously combining dread, veneration, and wonder that is inspired by authority or by the sacred or sublime."[2] In simple terms, awe is a reaction to something unknown—something fearful yet wonderful.

These days, this emotion is not something that is often used to describe a Christian religious experience. In fact, the younger

1. Ramsey, *Truth on Fire*, 32.
2. *Merriam-Webster Dictionary*, "Awe."

generation from Western countries is traveling to places like South America and India to find this sense of awe in temples and other spiritual practices. In this chapter, let's talk about why being awe-struck matters and how Christianity can be a fountain of awe, as it has been for millennia.

Awe: The Emotion That Lifts Us Beyond Ourselves

When you stand at a seaside cliff, and you see the waves crashing at the rocks, your brain stops processing, your sense of self disappears, the passage of time slows down, and you just stand there in awe. You are afraid, but you can't look away. You may know the scientific mechanism by which this happens, yet you still wonder *how*. All the problems you have been toiling over for weeks seem pointless and, frankly, silly.

When you hear a symphony so moving that it brings tears to your eyes, look up at a night sky decorated with stars, or listen to a story of heroism and self-sacrifice, something clicks inside you. You feel small, but not in a bad way. It's almost as if awe flips a switch inside your brain, creating space for wonder, humility, and joy.

Psychologists Monroy and Keltner say:

> Awe engages five processes—shifts in neurophysiology, a diminished focus on the self, increased prosocial relationality, greater social integration, and a heightened sense of meaning—that benefit well-being.[3]

And here's the thing: we *crave* these moments. It seems like it's in our *nature* to seek them out. We don't need medical practitioners to tell us it's good for us. The awe-seeking behavior is hardwired in us. We spend an absurd amount of money to be in hot air balloons watching the sunsets; we hike to mountaintops despite the apparent risks. Awe takes us outside of ourselves, makes us forget our egos, and reminds us there's more to this world.

---

3. Monroy and Keltner, "Awe as a Pathway," 309.

But *why*?

Why are we wired this way? Why do we long for awe in the first place? Is it just a by-product of our evolutionary heritage? If survival is the ultimate goal, how would the sense of awe help? If anything, don't we risk our lives in search of awe?

It's almost as if we were designed to look beyond ourselves—to be drawn to something greater.

This impression is so strong that even as an atheist, social psychologist Jonathan Haidt admits to the idea of humans having a God-shaped hole. He says:

> Many of my religious friends disagree about the origin of our God-shaped hole; they believe that the hole is there because we are God's creations and we long for our creator. But although we disagree about its origins, we agree about its implications: There is a hole, an emptiness in us all, that we strive to fill. If it doesn't get filled with something noble and elevated, modern society will quickly pump it full of garbage.[4]

Maybe awe is a feature, not a bug, pointing us toward something, *someone* greater than ourselves.

The Curious Minds

At the heart of awe lies mystery, the unknown. And we are wired to seek out the unknown. It's what drives us to explore, to ask questions, to push beyond what we can immediately see and understand. We want to go to Mars, to Jupiter. We explore outer space in search of life, in search of, well, *something*. Are we truly by ourselves in this vast universe? Is there anyone else out there? Mystery kindles our curiosity, and that curiosity isn't always tied to just the material world.

Maybe you have friends who are like this, or you yourself are one. Many of us claim to be "not religious" but still find ourselves drawn to spiritual ideas. In fact, the Pew Research Center found

---

4. Haidt, *Anxious Generation*, 215–16.

that 22 percent of US adults fall into this category of "spiritual but not religious."[5] That's a significant chunk of the population who may not attend a church, temple, synagogue, or mosque but still feel that there's something more out there.

And this desire is outwardly expressed in all sorts of ways. People go to psychics, hoping for insights into their future. Others rely on card reading, astrology, or crystals. There's a hunger for something beyond us, something unseen but deeply felt, not articulated but experienced.

Mark Matlock and the Barna Group studied this trend and found that about a quarter of US adults fall into the categories of "Curious Skeptics" or "Spiritually Curious."[6] These are people who find themselves drawn to questions about meaning, purpose, and the supernatural. Despite the significant cultural influence of its champions, naturalism (the belief that there is no supernatural world) is a minority, accounting for only 10 percent of the US adults in their study.[7]

Why do you think this is? Why are so many people still drawn to spiritual things in an age of scientific advancement and technological progress?

I think because deep down, we all know there's more to life.

We can't shake the feeling that we are part of something bigger. We might not always have the words to explain it, but we sense it. It's in those moments of awe that we feel a presence beyond ourselves. Our desire for noble causes, justice, compassion, and love—things that cannot be reduced down to evolutionary survival strategies, social constructs, or brain waves. You feel that life isn't just a series of random accidents.

Read the stories and watch the movies. Fantasy novels are filled with spiritual elements like prophecies and fate, and superhero movies move us with stories of self-sacrifice and duties. When Iron Man sacrifices himself, his arc is completed. He is redeemed. We are in *awe*.

5. Pew Research Center, "Spiritual but Not Religious."
6. Matlock, *Faith for the Curious*, 40.
7. Matlock, *Faith for the Curious*, 40.

The question isn't *whether* people are drawn to the feelings of awe. We are. The real question is *why*?

Maybe this built-in spiritual curiosity and awe-seeking tendency is a sign. Maybe we long for something beyond ourselves because there *is* something beyond ourselves. C. S. Lewis says:

> If I find in myself a desire which no experience in this world can satisfy, the most probable explanation is that I was made for another world. If none of my earthly pleasures satisfy it, that does not prove that the universe is a fraud. Probably earthly pleasures were never meant to satisfy it, but only to arouse it, to suggest the real thing.[8]

Christianity: The Wellspring of Awe

Now, we come to Christianity. Maybe you've been to a church before, and felt something: peaceful, happy, welcomed. But did you feel awe? Oftentimes, I find that awe and wonder have given way to accessibility and friendliness in our modern culture. Or maybe your experience was much more traditional, and you did feel a sense of awe. Whatever your experience may have been, it's important to note that Christianity has always been a wellspring of awe.

1. God Is Other and Unreachable

When you introduce yourself, what do you say? I say, "Hi, everyone, my name is So Ri, not *sorry*. I'm a Korean-Australian living in Sydney with my wife, Eojin, and my son, Noah." My introduction requires a few things that my identity *depends on*: the name that my parents gave me, my ethnic identity and nationality, my locality, and my relationships. Depending on who I'm talking to, I might even throw in my educational background and what I do for a living. All of these make up who I am.

---

8. Lewis, *Mere Christianity*, 136–37.

Now, let's compare this to how God introduces himself. This is when he appeared to Moses to call him to liberate the Israelites from slavery:

> God said to Moses, "I am *who I am.*" And he said, "Say this to the people of Israel: '*I am* has sent me to you.'" (Exod 3:14; emphasis added)

What an introduction! He doesn't need to say anything else. He is who he is. He does not depend on any descriptors or adjectives. He is the only one who truly stands independent.

Who is God? He is *other.* He is in a category by himself. He is *uncreated*; the rest are created. This means that everything relies on him for existence. Paul says this about Jesus: "For by him all things were created, in heaven and on earth, visible and invisible, whether thrones or dominions or rulers or authorities—*all things* were created through him and for him" (Col 1:16; emphasis added).

And Paul wasn't wrong to speak of Jesus in this way. Jesus himself said, "Truly, truly, I say to you, before Abraham was, *I am*" (John 8:58; emphasis added). Sound familiar? That's the same "I am" introduction that God used when he spoke to Moses. Jesus's self-proclamation as God was so loud and clear that those who heard him picked up stones to throw at him (John 8:59), as blasphemy was punishable by death in that culture.

Think about this otherness of God—the Creator of the universe. You may have been awestruck at the sight of thunderstorms or the crashing waves, but think about the one beyond. The one who created it all, who stands behind it all. King David sings, "The heavens declare the glory of God, and the sky above proclaims his handiwork" (Ps 19:1).

You see sports stars, scientists, and billionaires on television, and you might feel like they are so beyond you that you cannot compare with them. Multiply that feeling a thousand-fold, no, a million-fold, to infinity. Everyone, *everything*, is created. Only God stands beyond this category. He is *other.*

And because God is big and we are small, and he is in a category of his own, no wonder he is in a realm of the unknown.

Philosopher Immanuel Kant contrasts the noumenon: the thing in itself, in contrast to phenomenon: the thing as it appears to us.[9] Kant's idea was that we reason within the phenomenon and cannot reach the noumenon. In other words, God, as he truly is, remains beyond our grasp. We may perceive his creation and even his presence in ways that impact our lives (for example, the strong sense of moral obligations), but we cannot fully comprehend or reach him.

This idea of God-beyond-reach is well reflected in world religions. Many temples are built on top of mountains, out of reach from the everyday. This symbolizes a deeper spiritual truth: God is above, transcendent, and unreachable. It's no wonder that throughout history, humans have tried to bridge the gap—through sacrifices, rituals, and acts of devotion—taking extreme measures at times. Even in the Bible, we read about people building a very tall tower, the tower of Babel as it's commonly called, to reach God (Gen 11:1–9).

Yet, even as we recognize God's otherness, we also recognize something within ourselves—a desire for him. We are made in his image, and even though the fall has stained us, it has not erased that imprint. It's covered but not carved out. This is the Christian explanation for why we possess such a deep hunger for awe, a desire to behold something greater than ourselves. We climb mountains, marvel at the night skies, and stand in reverence before acts of heroism. All of these are echoes of a deeper reality, signposts for the one who is truly beyond.

So then, can't we just go to God? The problem is, even though we desire him, we cannot see him. It's not just that we lack the ability; it's also that we are undeserving of his presence because he is holy. Holy means set apart, and God is set apart in every way. He is light, and we are darkness. The two cannot coexist. When light shines, darkness disappears. When confronted with the holiness of God, prophet Isaiah said, "Woe is me! For I am lost; for I am a man of unclean lips, and I dwell in the midst of a people of unclean lips; for my eyes have seen the King, the LORD of hosts!" (Isa 6:4).

9. See Editors of Encyclopaedia Britannica, "Noumenon."

And when Jesus called Simon Peter, he fell to the ground and said, "Depart from me, for I am a sinful man, O Lord" (Luke 5:8).

Maybe you've experienced this before. You've met someone who is so different, better, and set apart that you feel less than. And you don't like that feeling. You want to hide. You don't want to be seen. This is precisely the feeling that the prophet and the disciple are experiencing, but only times that by an infinity. The holiness of God is a crushing weight to a sinner.

So, what hope is there? If God is truly other—unreachable and unapproachable—then why bother with this desire to search for him? Is this just an eternal torment, our punishment for rebellion? If the divide between Creator and creation is so vast, what can bridge the gap?

2. God Is Near and Personally Relatable

It would have been well within his right to stay afar. If the Creator decided he did not want to reveal himself to his creation, who could stop him? Could we pull him from underneath the desk he is hiding from? Could we search the forests, the deep sea, or outer space?

A few months ago, my wife and I were blessed with our son. He is so very cute but, frankly, helpless. He cries when he's hungry, uncomfortable, and sleepy. He can't even fall asleep by himself. We have to hold him in our arms to comfort him. He is *totally* dependent.

Now, in December every year, we celebrate a time when the God of the universe decided to come to us in such a way. The God who is other—who is so set apart from the rest of us, who is incomprehensible. The God who created the universe and everything in it, and the God who has all authority in the heavens and the earth. In his boundless love for us, he couldn't remain afar and came to us in human flesh. God who is *other*, became *near*.

Isaiah prophesied in the eighth century BC, "Therefore the Lord himself will give you a sign. Behold, the virgin shall conceive and bear a son, and shall call his name Immanuel" (Isa 7:14), and centuries later, a messenger of God revealed who this prophecy was pointing to:

> All this took place to fulfill what the Lord had spoken by the prophet: "Behold, the virgin shall conceive and bear a son, and they shall call his name Immanuel" (which means, *God with us*). (Matt 1:22–23; emphasis added)

Jesus is *God with us*. He is the embodiment of God's *otherness* harmonized with his passion for *nearness* to us. And this humility of God did not just mean he became human. Now, the Jews at the time were looking forward to the promised one who was coming with political power to overthrow the Roman Empire that was oppressing them.

But Jesus came as the son of a carpenter. He was born in a manger. He was a refugee in his early years. He was a second-class citizen in a land occupied by imperialist rulers, which meant he couldn't get a fair trial when he was framed, tortured, and killed for crimes he did not commit. Paul puts this beautifully in Phil 2:5–8:

> Have this mind among yourselves, which is yours in Christ Jesus, who, though he was in the form of God, did not count equality with God a thing to be grasped, but emptied himself, by taking the form of a servant, being born in the likeness of men. And being found in human form, he humbled himself by becoming obedient to the point of death, even death on a cross.

This is why he *gets us*. He knows our pains and our sufferings; he even knows our death. He is *near* us.

This nearness of God doesn't stop there. Jesus, as he completed his earthly ministry, sent the Helper, the Holy Spirit, to teach us and to remind us of the things Jesus has said (John 14:26). This is why Christians don't need psychics or *mediums* in the literal sense, because we have direct contact with *the* Spirit. This is why we're called the temple (1 Cor 3:16) and priests (1 Pet 2:9).

3. Experiencing Awe and Wonder Here and Now

Given this, is it any surprise that Christian life is full of awe and wonder? Belief in a God who created the universe with awesome power, who became near to us in wonderful humility and love, is our unceasing fountain.

When we go to church, we raise our hands in worship of this God in awe. The God who is worthy of all our praise. The God who deserves our loyalty and allegiance. Singing and adoring the same God with a diverse yet unified community of believers intensifies this experience.

I've already shared a shorter excerpt of this scene in a previous chapter, but it's worth quoting again. This is when John describes what he saw in a vision, of things to come:

> After this I looked, and behold, a great multitude that no one could number, from every nation, from all tribes and peoples and languages, standing before the throne and before the Lamb, clothed in white robes, with palm branches in their hands, and crying out with a loud voice, "Salvation belongs to our God who sits on the throne, and to the Lamb!" And all the angels were standing around the throne and around the elders and the four living creatures, and they fell on their faces before the throne and worshiped God, saying, "Amen! Blessing and glory and wisdom and thanksgiving and honor and power and might be to our God forever and ever! Amen." (Rev 7:9–12)

Doesn't this give you chills? People from every nation, tribe, and language will come before the throne of God, crying out at the top of their lungs. Not even the heavenly angels can bear the weight of God's glory and fall on their faces, awestruck.

This is the scene Christians think about (or at least *should* think about) when we gather at church week in and week out. What we do is a practice run, a preview, a trailer of a once-in-a-lifetime blockbuster movie.

But it's not only on Sundays that we experience awe. We also experience it in our daily lives.

I don't remember the exact date and time when I became a Christian. But there are a few things I do remember. The following Monday, after I committed my life to Jesus, I was daydreaming on a train to my university as a student and saw a few trees through the windows. As a nerdy biochemistry student, I would have normally used that opportunity to review my mental notes about the photosynthetic pathways and the Krebs cycle, but not that day. Instead, when sunlight broke through those branches, an overwhelming sense of awe filled me and tears welled up in my eyes.

Knowing God changed everything. All the things that I had passed by without giving a second thought were suddenly reasons to worship. Everything became a signpost pointing toward the true source. It was as if a curtain had been pulled aside, and I could see things for what they were for the first time.

Following these signposts to discover God and his beauty with child-like curiosity is what Christianity is about. As we're nearing the end of this short book, you may have gotten the impression that I have all the answers to the most difficult questions in life, but that's not true. And if anyone comes along and says they do, beware! Christianity doesn't present an exhaustive list of all answers in life; it presents a journey. Even after my dramatic transformation, I still discover who God is in nature, in the Bible, as I enjoy a good time with friends and struggle through the unsavory things in life. And if certain things don't make sense, I go to the source: God.

That brings us to the topic of prayer. In prayer, we experience the quiet presence of the divine. In these moments, God's nearness is felt. There are many stories in the Bible that demonstrate what prayer is about, but this one is my favorite. This is when the prophet Elijah flees persecution:

> There he came to a cave and lodged in it. And behold, the word of the LORD came to him, and he said to him, "What are you doing here, Elijah?" He said, "I have been very jealous for the LORD, the God of hosts. For the people of Israel have forsaken your covenant, thrown down your altars, and killed your prophets with the sword, and

I, even I only, am left, and they seek my life, to take it away." And he said, "Go out and stand on the mount before the LORD." And behold, the LORD passed by, and a great and strong wind tore the mountains and broke in pieces the rocks before the LORD, but the LORD was not in the wind. And after the wind an earthquake, but the LORD was not in the earthquake. And after the earthquake a fire, but the LORD was not in the fire. *And after the fire the sound of a low whisper.* And when Elijah heard it, he wrapped his face in his cloak and went out and stood at the entrance of the cave. And behold, there came a voice to him and said, "What are you doing here, Elijah?" (1 Kgs 19:9–13; emphasis added)

In these quiet moments of prayer, God listens and speaks. You may not hear him verbally like Elijah did in this story, but he speaks. The Holy Spirit who dwells in us reminds us of what Jesus has said and done.

When I'm upset at my wife for not meeting my needs, I pray. Then, the Spirit reminds me that I am to serve her and not expect to be served, just as Jesus came to serve, not to be served (Mark 10:45).

When I'm unsure about my career choices, I pray. The Spirit reminds me that whichever path I take, I should do it for the glory of God (1 Cor 10:31).

When I'm overwhelmed with shame, I pray. The Spirit reminds me of God's abundant love—to the point of sending Jesus to die for me *while* I was still a sinner (Rom 5:8)—and that I should always remember this grace.

When I'm anxious about the future, I pray. The Spirit reminds me that for those who love God, all things work together for good (Rom 8:28).

Christianity is not a set of instructions and rules that you can master and be done with. It's a walk with Jesus, *God with us*, until the very end. It's a wonderful journey where your desire for awe and wonder is continually satisfied.

This idea of journey is beautifully described in a literary masterpiece and one of the bestselling books in history, *The Pilgrim's*

Progress, written by John Bunyan and published in 1678. The story describes how a man named "Graceless" becomes "Christian" and journeys toward heaven.

What is so encouraging about the book is that the protagonist's journey to the point of him becoming Christian accounts for only one-tenth of the story. The rest is dedicated to what happens after, how he wrestles with and overcomes the obstacles with God's timely help.

Likewise, my faith as a Christian is a journey. I can never know *everything* there is to know about God—he is God, and I'm not. The wellspring of awe and wonder is a bottomless resource that continually satisfies my child-like curiosity as I walk with Jesus step by step.

A beautiful hymn written by a Canadian preacher and theologian, Albert B. Simpson, describes it well:

> 'Tis so sweet to walk with Jesus,
> Step by step and day by day;
> Stepping in His very footprints,
> Walking with Him all the way.
> Step by step, step by step,
> I would walk with Jesus,
> All the day, all the way,
> Keeping step with Jesus.[10]

Conclusion

It only takes a few moments of introspection to reveal our deep desires for awe and wonder. And these desires point to the one beyond.

When you recognize this sense of awe, I invite you to use that opportunity and take a fresh look at Christianity. Christianity reveals a God who is truly *other* who became *near*. Even when we didn't deserve him, he came near—to satisfy our restless hearts

---

10. Simpson, "Step by Step."

because there's a God-shaped hole in all of us that can never be filled by what this world offers.

Walking with Jesus opens the door to a profound experience of awe that no created thing—be it a breathtaking sunset or a captivating book—can truly satisfy. It brings peace and clarity that no psychic or palm reader can offer. Go to him and drink. He is the wellspring of life. Go and walk with him. He is who you need for your quest. He *is* the quest.

7

Christianity Is Happier
Than You Might Think

I think there must be something wrong with me, Linus. Christmas is
coming, but I'm not happy. I don't feel the way I'm supposed to feel.
—Charlie Brown[1]

WHEN I FIRST BECAME a Christian, my friends noticed. They didn't
say, "You're holier than before" or "You're more religious than before." Instead, they said, "You look happier." This is a lived experience for many Christians who understand the implications of the
Christian message.

Despite this, there is still a pervasive cultural caricature of
Christianity that portrays it as rigid, rules-based, and frankly, "not
so fun." This perception is particularly strong among the young,
who frequently view Christianity as a set of restrictions: don't do
this, don't do that. It creates an image of faith that is synonymous
with *denial*, suggesting that Christians are sacrificing precious moments of joy and happiness in the name of self-restraint.

1. Melendez, *Charlie Brown Christmas*, 1:39.

This is a problem because, in the end, everyone wants to be happy, right? We pursue a career to be happy, we build wealth to be happy. We start and nurture relationships to be happy. But if you believe Christianity is what stands between you and happiness, why would you choose Christianity? If it doesn't further your cause, why bother?

These are great questions that are worth serious attention. The first order of business, though, is this: what is "happiness" anyway?

What Is Happiness?

When you say you are happy or that you want to be happy, what do you mean? Commonly, we use it to mean a positive emotion we get when we get what we want. Unfortunately, we find that these emotions are short-lived. You may be thrilled when you get that dream job, but that feeling slowly runs dry. You are ecstatic when your favorite sports team wins the trophy, but that feeling quickly fades away when you go to work the next day.

Because of this, some distinguish happiness, the fleeting positive emotion that depends on external circumstances, from *joy*, the deeper emotion that comes from within.[2] But we also read academic articles such as the one by Laura Cottrell, who expertly performed a concept analysis and found this:

> Attributes of joy describe a spontaneous, sudden and transient concept associated with connection, awareness, and freedom. Attributes of happiness describe a pursued, long-lasting, stable mental state associated with virtue and self-control.[3]

So, who's right? Is happiness fleeting or long-lasting?

While semantics is a fascinating topic, we don't need to make a hasty call at this stage. Instead, we could easily take *Merriam-Webster*'s definition of happiness: "a state of well-being and contentment; a pleasurable or satisfying experience," which is

2. See Koller, "Happiness and Joy."
3. Cottrell, "Joy and Happiness," 1506.

synonymous with joy.[4] We can still appreciate and recognize different levels, degrees, and types of happiness.

And it's the long-lasting contentment that people are really after, isn't it? When we say, "Everyone wants to be happy," we don't mean, "Everyone wants to have spontaneous, sudden, and fleeting moments of positive emotions." Instead, we mean, "Everyone wants to have a long-lasting stable mental state of contentment and well-being." That's what we are after. But how do we get there?

How Do We Reach Happiness? The Christian Perspective

What makes you happy? Is it when you watch your favorite sports game or when you finally purchase your first home? Let's look at the Christian perspective on how we reach happiness.

1. Relationship with God

In the previous chapter, we discussed how Christianity provides a framework for a close relationship with God, who is *other* but *near*, who is a source of awe and wonder. Interestingly, scientists say that close relationships are what keep us happy.[5]

Then, putting the two together won't be too much of a logical jump. For Christians, this relationship with God is not just an abstract concept—it's a lived reality that provides deep, long-lasting happiness. A loving relationship with God brings a sense of security, belonging, and purpose.

Unlike human relationships, which can be fragile and temporary, a relationship with God is unshakable and eternal. No doubt you've been disappointed with people and betrayed by close friends. It doesn't matter how good your friends, spouse, or family members are; they are finite and limited. They may not have intended to hurt you, but they did, and they will! Therefore, putting

---

4. *Merriam-Webster Dictionary*, "Happiness."

5. Mineo, "Joy Is Better," para. 8.

your trust in them too much is a risky endeavor. The same applies the other way around, too; being on the receiving end of unrestricted and unwarranted trust can be draining, too high of a bar that no one can satisfy.

Not with God. He is strong and mighty. He is the unshakable rock that we can lean on. The Psalmist sings, "Trust in him at all times, O people; pour out your heart before him; God is a refuge for us" (Ps 62:8).

But merely believing that God exists is not enough—how we understand and relate to him matters deeply for our happiness. Studies have shown that different concepts of God can lead to different outcomes. For example, scientists have found that people with a benevolent image of God lead healthier lives,[6] but people with a negative image of God were more distressed and depressed.[7]

So, what is the Christian understanding of God? According to Christianity, God is, for all eternity, a community. The Father, the Son, and the Holy Spirit have been in a unique partnership even before anything was created. Relationships are not accidental but essential components of existence.

We also believe in the God of justice. Now, this may have contributed to many misconceptions of God as a judgmental figure who's constantly watching you so that he can punish your every misstep. But when you think about it, the fact that God is a just God means that he sets the boundaries and enforces them.

It's now widely accepted that not having boundaries is detrimental to children's development. The limitless freedom you give them tends to lead to uncertainty and anxiety.[8]

God has done what any good parent would do: set and enforce boundaries. We can have set expectations because we believe in a God of justice. This provides a stable foundation for our happiness.

There is a problem, though—our sins. Like a child throwing a tantrum, we decided that we don't like the boundaries that God

6. Krause et al., "Benevolent," 1515–16.

7. Schaap-Jonker et al., "Types of God Representations," 209.

8. Amen and Fay, *Raising Mentally Strong Kids*, 94.

has given us. Being so myopic, we didn't understand that it was for our protection.

Now, if we were to stop there, we wouldn't get happiness. Here lies the uniqueness of Christianity: grace. Through Jesus, believers are confident in God's unchanging love, not because of what we have done but because of what he has done—on that cross when the Son of God bore our punishment. Jesus paid our debt to restore our relationship with God.

This helps us rise beyond the shame and guilt and confidently approach God as his children. Paul says, "Therefore, since we have been justified by faith, we have *peace with God* through our Lord Jesus Christ" (Rom 5:1; emphasis added). This peace with God gives tremendous happiness that external circumstances cannot shake.

By the way, why do we get closer to happiness when we go deeper into the Christian understanding of God? Is this a "happy" coincidence, or maybe it's because this is the way it's supposed to be?

2. The Way It Is Supposed to Be

In a previous chapter, I discussed Plantinga's note on *shalom* or peace, or as he describes it, "the way things ought to be."[9] This means that God has created us with a specific design and purpose. When we deviate from this design, we face its consequences, just like the microwave with a metal spoon.

So, what was this purpose, this design? We talked about our design as the image of God before, and there is one more related point to make.

The Westminster Shorter Catechism (series of short questions and answers that summarize Christian principles) asks, "What is the chief end of man?" and the response is: "Man's chief end is to glorify God, and to enjoy him for ever."[10]

9. Plantinga, *Not the Way*, 10.
10. Westminster Assembly, "Shorter Catechism," §1.

This response is significant. According to Christianity, the very purpose of our being is joy. It's happiness. But it isn't saying that we should seek happiness *as the goal*. Instead, we are called to enjoy *him*. We are to reflect God's glory as *his* image. Christianity frees us from the often exhausting, self-focused pursuit of happiness by shifting our attention outward—toward God and his purpose.

This is a radical departure from the modern worldview, which tells us we must create or grasp happiness for ourselves. The world often frames happiness as something that can be accomplished through wealth, pleasure, self-improvement, and a sense of achievement for ourselves. But these pursuits leave us feeling empty when we realize that no amount of external achievement can satisfy the deepest longings of the soul. The ego is insatiable and nothing in this world quenches that thirst.

The biblical view is that these longings can only be satisfied when we restore "the way it's supposed to be" and look *outward*. Science seems to corroborate this view. One study found that self-centeredness is associated with fluctuating happiness (happiness that alternates between pleasure and displeasure) and selflessness with authentic-durable happiness.[11]

Christianity teaches self-sacrifice in this context. We sacrifice the self not *in spite* of joy but *because* of joy—the real joy. The author of Hebrews describes Jesus as "the founder and perfecter of our faith, who *for the joy* that was set before him endured the cross, despising the shame, and is seated at the right hand of the throne of God" (Heb 12:2; emphasis added).

Jesus looked toward joy on the cross. The joy of finishing the work. The joy of demonstrating the true image of God. The joy of making peace and restoring God's order in this world. It's for the *joy* he endured the cross.

You go to the gym and push yourself to the limit. Why? There is joy set before you. You change the wet and dirty diapers of your children day and night. Why? There is joy set before you. In the same way, when I spent precious weekday nights going to the

---

11. Dambrun, "Self-Centeredness and Selflessness," 10.

streets to share the gospel with others, sure, there were times when I didn't want to do it—but there was joy. When I go to church every week, there is a joy to be discovered in engaging with a fellow community. When I consciously do the right thing following Jesus's example, even when it's inconvenient, there is joy.

Christians may seem like we're sacrificing "fun" for religiosity, but far from it, we're actually sacrificing "fun" for "greater fun." Jesus used this analogy:

> The kingdom of heaven is like treasure hidden in a field, which a man found and covered up. Then in his *joy* he goes and sells all that he has and buys that field. (Matt 13:44; emphasis added)

Just imagine how his family and friends would have reacted when, out of nowhere, he came home and started to *joyfully* sell everything he had! They would have thought he had gone crazy! If only they had seen the treasure too.

Similarly, when Jesus called his disciples, they "left the boat and their father and followed him" (Matt 4:22). Now, I'm not telling you to close this book, sell everything you own, and donate it to a local church. All I'm saying is that when we discover that treasure, the beauty of Jesus, we *radically reprioritize* our lives to put him first because he is worth it. We sacrifice joy, the joy for ourselves, for *greater joy*, the joy in him.

3. Come and Learn from Me

Who do you think was the happiest person in history? If we're going by the approach to happiness above, who was the person who fulfilled their design and purpose the most, the true image of God? Who was the person who set their eyes on the ultimate joy set before him? You guessed it! It was Jesus.

So, shouldn't we go to him for advice on happiness? Shouldn't we learn from the expert? Fortunately for us, he gave us a series of teachings specifically about happiness. You may have heard of them, even if you're not a Christian. It's called the Beatitudes, a series of statements that start with "blessed are." The Greek word *makarios* is translated to "blessed" in English, but it also means "happy."[12] So, what did Jesus say about happiness?

> Blessed are the poor in spirit, for theirs is the kingdom of heaven. Blessed are those who mourn, for they shall be comforted. Blessed are the meek, for they shall inherit the earth. Blessed are those who hunger and thirst for righteousness, for they shall be satisfied. Blessed are the merciful, for they shall receive mercy. Blessed are the pure in heart, for they shall see God. Blessed are the peacemakers, for they shall be called sons of God. Blessed are those who are persecuted for righteousness' sake, for theirs is the kingdom of heaven. Blessed are you when others revile you and persecute you and utter all kinds of evil against you falsely on my account. Rejoice and be glad, for your reward is great in heaven, for so they persecuted the prophets who were before you. (Matt 5:3–11)

Now, have a read of it again, but in your mind, replace the "Blessed are" with "Happy are." What do you think? How does it compare with the modern narrative of happiness?

Happy are the poor, not the rich in spirit. Happy are those who mourn, not those who are always joyful. Happy are the meek, not the proud. Happy are those who hunger and thirst for righteousness, not those who hunger and thirst for self-interest. Happy are the merciful, not the ruthless. Happy are the pure in heart, not the ones who "follow their heart." Happy are the peacemakers, not the ones who shy away from difficult situations out of inconvenience. Happy are those who are persecuted for righteousness's sake, not those who enjoy comfort at the expense of what's right.

It's so important to remember, however, that these aren't just ethical instructions that we are meant to follow whether we like it or not. Before they are *prescriptions*, these are *descriptions*.

Descriptions of who? Who else but Jesus himself?

---

12. McLoughlin, "Happiness and Well-Being," 78.

Jesus was poor in spirit. Despite being God, he emptied himself and pronounced dependency on the Father (Phil 2:6–8).

Jesus mourned for Lazarus, his friend (John 11:35), and for Jerusalem (Luke 19:41). He sympathizes with our weaknesses (Heb 4:15).

Jesus was meek. Despite having all authority, he came to serve, not to be served (Matt 20:28).

Jesus hungered and thirsted for righteousness. When he said, "I thirst" on the cross (John 19:28), it showed his ultimate desire for righteousness, making things right with God.

Jesus is merciful. He was the friend of sinners and tax collectors (Matt 11:19), embraced the social outcasts (Luke 17:11–19), and ultimately showed mercy to us, sinners, by taking the penalty of our sins in our place.

Jesus is pure in heart. He is sinless (Heb 4:15) and has an undivided heart for God's purpose.

Jesus is the peacemaker. He reconciled us to God (Col 1:19–20) through his work on the cross.

Jesus was the ultimate sufferer for righteousness, unjustly condemned, mocked, and crucified (Matt 26–27).

Christians are not called to follow the "eight easy steps to happiness." We are not called to *obey the rules*. Instead, we are called to *follow a person*. We are called to follow Jesus. He says:

> Come to me, all who labor and are heavy laden, and I will give you rest. Take my yoke upon you, and learn from me, for I am gentle and lowly in heart, and you will find rest for your souls. For my yoke is easy, and my burden is light. (Matt 11:28–30)

Notice what he says. He doesn't say, "Oh, you are heavy laden; I'll remove your burden so you can relax and be happy." Instead, he says, "Take my yoke upon you."

Happiness is not having the total freedom to do whatever we want to do, with no limits to our desires. Happiness is not being completely free of worries, concerns, or suffering in this life. Happiness comes from being yoked with the right person, Jesus.

When my wife and I got married, we put a yoke upon ourselves. I'm bound to her, and she is bound to me—not just metaphorically but also legally. Does that give me less joy and happiness because I'm now less *free*? Not at all! Having boundaries gives me *more* freedom.

I'm free from my desire to find the perfect person; I've found her. I'm free from the anxiety of not being loved by everyone; I'm loved by the person who matters most. I'm free from running around searching for my heart's content; I've found rest at home.

In the same way, when we are yoked with Christ, we are *truly* free. We can *truly* find rest, rest from our self-centeredness, rest from being the hero of the story. We can trust him completely. He's the only one who can bear such a burden because he is God, he is man, and because he died for our sins, and he lives as a victorious King.

I don't mean that in the sense of movies where a character close to the story passes away and the protagonist somberly says, "I know he lives on, in my heart," or "I know he is here with me in spirit." And I don't look to Jesus as I look to heroic historical figures, admiring and trying to live by his example as best I can.

Instead, I look to Jesus as the risen Lord, alive today, having authority over all things, and intimately present in my life. He didn't leave us to our own devices but sent the Holy Spirit to help us, guide us, and transform us from within.

Because of this, Christianity isn't about striving to attain happiness on our own—it's about living in joyful dependence on him, the source of all happiness. To be yoked to Christ is not a burden; it's the greatest freedom, the deepest rest, and the truest happiness we can ever know.

Conclusion

Happiness that Christianity promises isn't about feeling good or having fun all the time. It's about something deeper, something more grounded, something that lasts even through life's tragedies.

Christianity isn't about enforcing rules to joylessly follow—it's about stepping into the kind of life we were meant to live and discovering our original purpose. It's about having a relationship with the God who loves us despite our failures. It's about finding peace in a way that doesn't depend on how many assets you own, your mood, or your reputation.

Jesus wasn't another spiritual teacher handing out self-help advice or a guru with enlightening yet elusive messages. He didn't say, "Here's the secret to happiness—go and try." Instead, he said, "Come to me." He invites us into a relationship with him. In him, we find something the world can't offer: *deep* rest, *lasting* peace, and *true* happiness.

It's not an empty promise of life without any difficulties or hardships, but a sure guarantee of true happiness *in spite of* them, enabling us to patiently and joyfully look forward to the day when Jesus restores all things. John says:

> He will wipe away every tear from their eyes, and death shall be no more, neither shall there be mourning, nor crying, nor pain anymore, for the former things have passed away. (Rev 21:4)

Until then, we just have to be yoked with the right person as we march through the unavoidable journey of life.

Jesus is not a historical figure we reminisce about. He is the risen King. Go to him and find deep rest. Walk with him and find true happiness.

8

Christianity Is Better Than You Might Think
What's Next?

This hill, though high, I do long to ascend;
To me the difficulty won't offend.
For I perceive the way to life lies here:
Come pluck up, heart, let's neither faint nor fear;
Better, though difficult, the right way to go,
Than wrong, though easy, where the end is woe.—Christian[1]

Now, WE ARE AT the end of this short book, so let's remind ourselves what I said at the beginning: "As a fellow traveler, I want to introduce to you the path I'm on. My goal is to help you see the path clearly, dispel the myths, address the objections, and uncover the heart of Christianity—its truth, goodness, and beauty."

So, are we there yet?

---

1. Bunyan, *Pilgrim's Progress*, 30.

Maybe you can now see that Christianity is more reasonable, more relevant, more inclusive, more diverse, more awesome, and happier than you had first thought, and you're ready to take the next step. Congratulations!

Or, maybe you're halfway there, but you want the extra bit of *certainty*. You can now see where Christians are coming from and empathize with the internal logic, but you are not ready to take the next step because you see the implications—what it *costs*. Jesus said:

> Whoever does not bear his own cross and come after me cannot be my disciple. For which of you, desiring to build a tower, does not first sit down and count the cost, whether he has enough to complete it? Otherwise, when he has laid a foundation and is not able to finish, all who see it begin to mock him, saying, "This man began to build and was not able to finish." Or what king, going out to encounter another king in war, will not sit down first and deliberate whether he is able with ten thousand to meet him who comes against him with twenty thousand? And if not, while the other is yet a great way off, he sends a delegation and asks for terms of peace. So therefore, any one of you who does not renounce all that he has cannot be my disciple. (Luke 14:27–33)

What does he mean? He means we need to understand what's involved in following him. Being a Christian is not just about intellectual assent; it's a lifelong devotion. It's not just about acknowledging that Jesus exists or might have existed as a historical figure—it's about orienting your entire life in service of the risen King.

It involves repentance—turning away from *your* path, *your* way—and faith—trusting in *his* path, *his* way. Think of repentance not as an abstract religious concept but as a real, practical transformation. It's humbly admitting you've been walking in the wrong direction and turning around. Faith, then, is stepping forward on that new path, even if you don't yet see the finish line, because you trust and treasure the person you're holding onto.

So, no wonder you want certainty—you want a *guarantee* that this is worth your devotion and commitment. If the cost is this big, you want the peace of mind that this is indeed the right path, even when you recognize the unquestionable benefits. If this is you, maybe an illustration will help.

You wake up one morning and check the weather app. There's a 70 percent chance of heavy rain throughout the day. You let out a sigh but muster up the courage to get out of bed, get ready, and head to work. You take an umbrella with you despite not having the absolute certainty that it will rain. Sure, if it doesn't rain, you'll have carried the umbrella all day for no reason. But if it does, you'll be glad you brought it.

See, we live by faith all the time—Christian and non-Christian alike. Every day, we make informed decisions even when we don't have unquestionable proof. We weigh the evidence, consider the costs, assess the benefits, and then *act*. We have to! Faith in Christ is no different. At some point, you have to say, "I've done my research; it's time to act." In Jesus's analogy, when a man discovered treasure in a field, he acted—*joyfully* selling *everything* he owned to buy that field (Matt 13:44).

And here's the thing—no one knows how much time they have. You might think you have all the time in the world to delay your decision to follow Jesus, but who knows what will happen in a month, a week, or even a day? Is today the time to act for you? Will you have your umbrella ready when it rains? Or will you blame the forecast for not saying 100 percent?

I mentioned the book *The Pilgrim's Progress* before. In it, the protagonist journeys through life, meeting different people along the way. Some try to trick him and lead him on the wrong path, and others encourage him to keep going. But in the end, that is *his* journey. Likewise, this is *yours*. No one else can walk this journey for you. The ball is in your court.

So, what will it be?

I pray that you will see Jesus for who he is: the *logos* who doesn't demand blind faith but offers *reasonable evidence* to follow him; the risen King who is not abstract and inconsequential but *present* and *relevant* in all aspects of your life; the merciful Lord who opens his arms to *everyone*, who died for us *while* we were still sinners; the second person of the Trinity who is the very foundation for our *diversity* and *unity*; the wellspring of *awe* and *wonder* who never runs dry, who never keeps us in the dark; the true source of happiness who for the *joy* of *you* joining his kingdom endured the cross.

Go to him. He is the one you've been searching for.

Go to him in prayer. Open your heart and share with him your doubts, your wants, and your needs—your need of him. Admit your brokenness and your helplessness. He is mighty and able—only he can rescue.

Go to him in the Bible. Start by discovering the riches and beauty of his words and actions in the four Gospels—Matthew, Mark, Luke, and John. Let him speak to your soul as he whispers his love, calls you to trust, and commands your allegiance.

And when you do, don't do it alone. Find a local church that faithfully teaches the Bible, a group of people united in him. The church isn't just a building or a Sunday morning ritual; it's a community of believers. Yes, this is your journey, but what good is a journey without companions? What good is a body without all its members?

I long for the day we'll meet in heaven and talk about our journeys. We'll sit together and recount the moments of doubt, discovery, and grace that led us home. We'll celebrate God's incredible work—the work that turned out to be *far, far* better than any of us might have first thought.

Bibliography

Africa Study Bible. "The History of Christianity in Africa." *The Gospel Coalition Africa*, Nov. 13, 2019. https://africa.thegospelcoalition.org/article/history-christianity-africa/.

Amen, Daniel G., and Charles Fay. *Raising Mentally Strong Kids*. Carol Stream, IL: Tyndale, 2024.

Athanasius. *On the Incarnation*. Translated by John Behr. Yonkers, NY: St. Vladimir's Seminary Press, 2011.

Bunyan, John. *The Pilgrim's Progress*. Abridged Christian Classics. Uhrichsville, OH: Barbour, 2010.

Cachiaras, Ben. "A Movement Away from Denominationalism: What's It Mean for Us?" *Christian Standard*, May 1, 2023. https://christianstandard.com/2023/05/a-movement-away-from-denominationalism-whats-it-mean-for-us/.

Childers, Alisa, and Tim Barnett. *The Deconstruction of Christianity: What It Is, Why It's Destructive, and How to Respond*. Carol Stream, IL: Tyndale, 2023.

Clines, David J. A. "The Image of God in Man." *Tyndale Bulletin* 19.1 (1968) 94.

Cottrell, Laura. "Joy and Happiness: A Simultaneous and Evolutionary Concept Analysis." *Journal of Advanced Nursing* 72.7 (2016) 1506–17. https://doi.org/10.1111/jan.12980.

Craig, William Lane. *Reasonable Faith: Christian Truth and Apologetics*. 3rd ed. Wheaton, IL: Crossway, 2008.

Dambrun, Michael. "Self-Centeredness and Selflessness: Happiness Correlates and Mediating Psychological Processes." *PeerJ* 5 (2017) e3306. https://doi.org/10.7717/peerj.3306.

Dickson, John. "The Purpose of Genesis 1: An Historical Approach." Centre for Public Christianity, Mar. 9, 2009. https://publicchristianity.org/article/the-purpose-of-genesis-1-an-historical-approach/.

The Editors of Encyclopaedia Britannica. "Khmer Rouge." *Encyclopedia Britannica*, Feb. 26, 2025. https://www.britannica.com/topic/Khmer-Rouge.

———. "Noumenon." *Encyclopedia Britannica*, Mar. 10, 2020. https://www.britannica.com/topic/noumenon.

Haidt, Jonathan. *The Anxious Generation: How the Great Rewiring of Childhood Is Causing an Epidemic of Mental Illness*. London: Allen Lane, 2024.

Johnson, Todd M. "Christianity Is Fragmented—Why?" Gordon Conwell Theological Seminary, Nov. 6, 2019. https://www.gordonconwell.edu/blog/christianity-is-fragmented-why/.

Keller, Timothy. *Galatians for You*. London: The Good Book Company, 2013.

———. "The Importance of Hell." Redeemer Churches and Ministries, 2009. https://www.redeemer.com/redeemer-report/article/the_importance_of_hell.

Kim, Wook-Dong. *Translations in Korea: Theory and Practice*. Singapore: Palgrave Macmillan, 2019.

Koller, Tessa. "The Fundamental Difference Between Happiness and Joy: How You Can Enrich Your Days With Joy." Medium, May 11, 2024. https://medium.com/@tessakoller/the-fundamental-difference-between-happiness-and-joy-5ea138ca83c6.

Krause, Neal, et al. "Benevolent Images of God, Gratitude, and Physical Health Status." *Journal of Religion and Health* 54 (2015) 1503–19. https://doi.org/10.1007/s10943-015-0063-0.

Leading Britain's Conversation. "Richard Dawkins: I'm a Cultural Christian." YouTube video, 8:10. Apr. 1, 2024. https://www.youtube.com/watch?v=COHgEFUFWyg.

Lewis, C. S. "Is Theology Poetry?" Samizdat University Press, 2014. https://www.samizdat.qc.ca/arts/lit/Theology=Poetry_CSL.pdf.

———. *Mere Christianity*. London: William Collins, 2012.

Martinón-Torres, María, et al. "Earliest Known Human Burial in Africa." *Nature* 593 (2021) 95–100. https://doi.org/10.1038/s41586-021-03457-8.

Matlock, Mark. *Faith for the Curious: How an Era of Spiritual Openness Shapes the Way We Live and Help Others Follow Jesus*. Grand Rapids: Baker, 2024.

McLoughlin, David. "Happiness and Well-Being in Christianity." In *Religious and Non-Religious Perspectives on Happiness and Wellbeing*, edited by Sharada Sugirtharajah, 78–94. London: Routledge, 2022.

Melendez, Bill, dir. *A Charlie Brown Christmas*. Lee Mendelson Film Productions and Bill Melendez Productions, 1965. Apple TV+.

Merriam-Webster Dictionary. "Awe." https://www.merriam-webster.com/dictionary/awe.

———. "Happiness." https://www.merriam-webster.com/dictionary/happiness.

Mineo, Liz. "Good Genes Are Nice, but Joy Is Better." *The Harvard Gazette*, Apr. 11, 2017. https://news.harvard.edu/gazette/story/2017/04/over-nearly-80-years-harvard-study-has-been-showing-how-to-live-a-healthy-and-happy-life/.

Monroy, Maria, and Dacher Keltner. "Awe as a Pathway to Mental and Physical Health." *Perspectives on Psychological Science* 18.2 (2022) 309–20. https://doi.org/10.1177/17456916221094856.

Morris, James H. "Rereading the Evidence of the Earliest Christian Communities in East Asia During and Prior to the Táng Period." *Missiology* 45.3 (2017) 252–64. https://doi.org/10.1177/0091829616685352.

Newton, Isaac. *Newton's Principia: The Mathematical Principles of Natural Philosophy by Sir Isaac Newton.* Translated by Andrew Motte. n.p.: Bill Stone Services, 2020. Kindle.

Nietzsche, Friedrich. *The Gay Science: With a Prelude in German Rhymes and an Appendix of Songs.* Edited by Bernard Williams, translated by Josefine Nauckhoff and Adrian Del Caro. Cambridge: Cambridge University Press, 2001.

———. *Thus Spake Zarathustra: A Book for All and None.* Translated by Thomas Common. Project Gutenberg, Dec. 1, 1999. https://www.gutenberg.org/ebooks/1998.

Nintendo. "The Legend of Zelda." Nintendo Entertainment System. 1986.

Peterson, Ryan S. "Image as Identity." In *The Imago Dei as Human Identity: A Theological Interpretation,* 53–83. University Park, PA: Penn State University Press, 2016. https://doi.org/10.5325/j.ctv1bxhojj.

Pew Research Center. "Key Findings from the Global Religious Futures Project." Dec. 21, 2022. https://www.pewresearch.org/religion/2022/12/21/key-findings-from-the-global-religious-futures-project/.

———. "5. Who Are 'Spiritual but Not Religious' Americans?" In *Spirituality Among Americans.* Dec. 7, 2023. https://www.pewresearch.org/religion/2023/12/07/who-are-spiritual-but-not-religious-americans/.

Plantinga, Cornelius, Jr. *Not the Way It's Supposed to Be: A Breviary of Sin.* Grand Rapids: Eerdmans, 1996.

Ramsey, Adam. *Truth on Fire.* London: The Good Book Company, 2021.

Rana, Fazale, and Hugh Ross. *Origins of Life: Biblical and Evolutionary Models Face Off.* Covina, CA: Reasons To Believe Press, 2014. Kindle.

Schaap-Jonker, Hanneke, et al. "Types of God Representations and Mental Health: A Person-Oriented Approach." *The International Journal for the Psychology of Religion* 27.4 (2017) 199–214. https://doi.org/10.1080/1050 8619.2017.1382119.

Simpson, Albert B. "Step by Step." 1897. https://hymnary.org/hymn/CYBER/6334.

Taylor, Samuel J. "Deconstruction and Disidentification: An Analysis of U.S. White Millennials' Exodus from Organized Evangelical Christianity." PhD diss., Ohio University, 2024.

Thiessen, Elmer John. *The Ethics of Evangelism: A Philosophical Defence of Ethical Proselytizing and Persuasion.* Milton Keynes: Paternoster, 2011. Kindle.

Voth, Jeff, and Jesse Muller. *Living in the Text: Becoming People of the Book.* Eugene, OR: Wipf & Stock, 2025.

Watkin, Christopher. *Biblical Critical Theory.* Grand Rapids: Zondervan Academic, 2022.

The Westminster Assembly. "Westminster Shorter Catechism." The Westminster Standard, Mar. 10, 2016. https://thewestminsterstandard.org/westminster-shorter-catechism/.

Wilkin, Jen, and J. T. English. *You Are a Theologian.* Brentwood, TN: B&H. 2023.

Wilson, James. "Nietzsche and Equality." In *Nietzsche and Ethics,* edited by Gudrun von Tevenar, 211–31. Bern: Peter Lang, 2007.

Zurlo, Gina A., et al. "World Christianity and Religions 2022: A Complicated Relationship." *International Bulletin of Mission Research* 46.1 (2021) 71–80. https://doi.org/10.1177/23969393211046993.

www.ingramcontent.com/pod-product-compliance
Lightning Source LLC
Chambersburg PA
CBHW070515090426
42735CB00012B/2794